BAAAD SHEEP

WHEN GOD'S PEOPLE LET YOU DOWN

ELLEN GILLETTE

CarePoint Ministries ❖ *Atlanta*
www.ChristianCarePoint.org

CarePoint Ministries, Inc.
www.CarePointMinistry.org
Atlanta, GA USA

CarePoint titles are available at discounts in bulk quantities. For details, contact the publisher at the above address.

Printed and Manufactured in the United States of America

Important Note: If at any time you feel you need to speak with a pastoral or professional Christian counselor, please call the church office for a referral to a member of our pastoral staff or a licensed professional Christian counselor. Church telephone number:

_____

For David:
the most Christ-like person in my life.

"[She] who has been forgiven much, loves much."
(Luke 7:47, author's paraphrase)

Acknowledgements

Any book is more than words on a page, more than pages within a binding. Books represent the culmination of events—both good and baaad!—in the lives of their authors, plus the culmination of events in the lives of all who took part in the writing, editing, and publishing processes. Further behind the scenes is our Creator God, "work(ing) for the good of those who love him who have been called according to his purpose" (Romans 8:28). I acknowledge him first and foremost, praying that he will be glorified through this workbook and in the lives of those who read it.

My husband David, daughters Terri and Becky, son-in-law Randy, and three grandchildren (Jasmine, Adam II, and baby Randy) patiently waited for me to exit my "shed" and resume whatever writing had interrupted—supper, playing, babysitting, weeding the garden, feeding the goats, etc. Their loving support means more than they could ever imagine.

From many miles away, our son Caleb, my parents, sister, and other family members and friends consistently act as "balcony people," cheering me on my way. I can only hope to be as encouraging to them as they are to me. Our youngest child, Adam, is in that "great cloud of witnesses" (Hebrews 12:1) as I run with perseverance (and a fair amount of complaining) the race God has set for me. As I cope with living in an Adam-less world, I am thankful for the comfort that assurance brings.

Thank you, Dr. Ken Dalton, for your encouragement, insight, and technical assistance. Thanks also to my brothers and sisters in Christ at Crossroads Church in Lillington, North Carolina, who prayed me through the process and kept asking, "So, how's the book coming?" Scott, Kelly, and the committed people at CarePoint recognized the seed of an idea from a brief online note and provided the soil in which it could germinate and blossom. I am grateful.

I have, at times (at many, many times), needed the love, mercy, and forgiveness of people I have hurt badly. I'd like to take this opportunity to extend the same to those who have hurt me. This workbook wouldn't have been possible without all the "baaad sheep" I've known (or heard about) over the years. "'You intended to harm...but God intended it for good to accomplish what is now being done...'" (Genesis 50:20). Be released from your guilt in the name of Jesus. And please..."'Go and sin no more'" (John 8:11b, NLT).

Contents

Preface

Our family of six lived in India for most of 1987 working with Youth With A Mission (YWAM). While there, a national told us that there were three religious groups in his country, each one with its own reputation. "The Muslims are known for their lust; the Hindus, their deception. And Christians," he said sadly, "are known for stabbing each other in the back." Undoubtedly, the actions of the *minority* of believers had poisoned the opinion of outsiders as to the character of the *majority*.

Let's call them *baaad* sheep.

As we look at these *baaad* sheep, we should remind ourselves that the "minority factor" is true for us as well. We've probably known hundreds of Christians during our lives. Only a small percentage, I trust, has hurt us. But hurt us they have. We want to look at some of the general areas in which we have been (or are being) let down by God's people, focusing on behavior that is in conflict with his commands.

The sessions won't cover every potential brand of *baaad* sheep, obviously, and the problems we'll address are not always discernible at the beginning of a church relationship. New members don't introduce themselves by saying, "Hi, I'm Billie Jean and I struggle with gossip" or "Thank you for welcoming me as your new pastor. Over the next ten years I will molest three of your teens, seduce two married women, and leave my family for the secretary."

When God seals us with the Holy Spirit as we put our trust in Jesus, he doesn't add a tattoo of our particular areas of weakness for all to see…and aren't you glad? If he did, however, everyone would be warned, would know better how to pray for us, and could even avoid us if necessary. We would see others the same way. That's just not the way it works. We learn to recognize/respond to *baaad* sheep through experience, discernment, and (hopefully) through studies such as this one.

According to Pat Zukeran, in his article entitled "Abusive Churches", he lists (combined with information from Dr. Ronald Enroth's book, *Churches That Abuse*) several characteristics of abusive churches:

> *First, abusive churches have a control-oriented style of leadership. Second, the leaders of such churches often use manipulation to gain complete submission from their members. Third, there is a rigid, legalistic lifestyle involving numerous requirements and minute details for daily life. Fourth, these churches tend to change their names often, especially once they are exposed by the media. Fifth, denouncing other churches is common because they see themselves as superior to all other churches. Sixth, these churches have a persecution complex and view themselves as being persecuted by the world, the media, and other Christian churches. Seventh, abusive churches specifically target young adults between eighteen and twenty-five years of age. The eighth and final mark of abusive churches is the great difficulty members have in getting out of or leaving these churches, a process often marked by social, psychological, or emotional pain.[1]*

These characteristics are significant to the problem of church abuse, and will certainly be addressed in this workbook, but our primary focus will be the more subtle ways churches abuse through their members or faithful attenders...primarily believers...as was the case for Karen (Leininger) King, who wrote a paper entitled "Healed of Church Abuse" for *Communion with God Ministries*. Her willingness to share freely about her journey through pain and beyond can inspire us on our own journey:

> *I felt hopeless, alienated, and that God really didn't care for me anymore. The past controlled my present and gave me a black, bleak looking future. These wounds were all inflicted by "Christians" and the Church. Maybe that is one reason it all seemed so much worse for me. Where I should have found love and support, I received criticism, judgment, condemnation, hurt, and loss of identity. While studying, it was a relief to find out that it wasn't just myself digging up these past hurts, but that it was Christ gently bringing these events to my consciousness so that He could touch me and give me inner healing.[2]*

In this workbook, we will look at our own hurts and learn ways to deal with them in a godly way through the healing touch of Christ. We will also learn how to avoid being *baaad* sheep ourselves.

Introduction

> *"'A new command I give you: Love one another. As I have loved you, so you must love one another. By this all men will know that you are my disciples, if you love one another.'"*
>
> *—John 13:34-35*

Welcome & Purpose

Welcome to the *Baaad Sheep* support group designed with compassion to approach the topic of church abuse. The purpose of the group is:

to share the love, grace, and mercy of Christ Jesus with each other by sharing and bearing each other's burdens, expressing our love and care for one another, and encouraging each other so that we might find hope, joy, value, and renewed life.

Opening Prayer

Father, we come together in the name of Jesus Christ, asking you to draw us closer to you, closer to one another, and closer to Christ who is the way, the truth, and the life. In his name we pray. Amen.

Meeting & Greeting

Although the workbook (with or without the accompaniment CD) may be beneficial on an individual basis, readers will almost certainly gain insight from the input of others in a small group format. I suggest handing out books at your initial meeting with plans for each member to read a particular session (or part of a session) before the next meeting rolls around. Discussion questions could be addressed at that time.

There are also homework assignments for personal application.

Take a few minutes to introduce yourselves and go over the sample covenant agreement which will be provided by your group leader. It is important for members of any small group to feel safe sharing with one another, confident that confidences will remain just that. To paraphrase a trendy thought, what happens in Group, stays in Group. Some of what you will discuss during the course of *Baaad Sheep* deals with sensitive issues. It would be wise to establish safety levels before that time.

The Gospel, Reader's Digest Condensed Version

Since love is the fulfillment of the Law (Romans 13:10), did you ever wonder why God didn't just periodically, post-Creation, send out a flier to everyone on the planet that read:

Love one another.

Just think of all the time that could have been saved! Moses might have spent forty *minutes* on Mount Sinai. And after thousands of years of God's singular message being repeated over and over, the church (and please note that when I say "the church" I mean the universal body of believers, not a particular one) would be exactly what he always intended it to be.

Yeah, right.

God went to extreme lengths to "flesh out" the radical concept of loving one another in the Bible. But just as a three-word flier was not adequate to fully explain his will, this workbook can't come close to revealing everything about the present state of affairs in the church today. Rather, it is intended to help you—by engaging in a group study discussion—"walk out" what God's *Word* teaches. If the world will only know (believe, be convinced of, buy into the whole idea) that we are Christians by our love *for one another,* it seems important that we learn to actually *do* it.

Biblical Blemish Cream

What will we *not* be addressing? For one thing, we won't be talking about the hurts of the world, which are vast. I would encourage the group to avoid getting bogged down by "bad-boss" stories and the like. Handling these hurts is a valid issue—by all means, learn to forgive the world's scoundrels too!—but our study's focus is Christians. The church needs to be accountable for its part in turning hurting people away from its doors and from the Lord—one particularly disastrous result of being "*baaad* sheep."

(That reminds me of the stand-up comedian who left a gig, only to be accosted by an angry little group that had caught his performance. "We're Christians," one of the group sputtered, "and we were highly offended by the way you talked about Christianity."

The comedian just smiled. "So forgive me."

(Out of the mouths of babes and buffoons….)

Jesus' teaching is clear: in the world, there's going to be trouble, that starts with T, that rhymes with P, which stands for People (John 16:33, with apologies to *The Music Man* lyricist Meredith Willson). Fallen man cannot help but reflect his spiritual depravity through word and deed. What we want to look at is the pervasive trouble within the body of Christ, also referred to as the church, the bride of Christ, the New Jerusalem, and the wife of the Lamb (see Revelation 21).

Paul wrote of Christ giving himself up for the church "to make her holy, cleansing her by the washing with water through the word, and to present her to himself as a radiant church, without stain or wrinkle or any other blemish, but holy and blameless" (Ephesians 5:26-27). There is so much pain within the Body—so much *Christian-generated* pain—that I find it difficult to believe that Jesus' return is imminent…an Extreme Makeover is still very much in progress with his bride.

We are also not going to discuss the actions of everyone at church whose behavior is suspect. There is, at any given time, a number of different groups within any given congregation, including people who have not formally committed to a relationship with Jesus Christ. They are raw material, not yet submitted to the Lord's pruning shears.

One Sunday after the newspaper, which ran my weekly column, printed a story about a local bar's contest for the Sexiest Sounding Woman, a lady approached me at church, tight-lipped with righteous indignation. "Can't you do something?" She was offended that the article appeared in the…*secular*…press.

Another time, I observed with chagrin as a women's jail ministry team member confronted a regular worship service attendee over her choice of clothing—far too revealing for the woman's sensitive tastes. In jail! A non-believer!

At church, there are...or should be, if we are evangelizing our community well...unsaved people in our midst. It would be pointless, fruitless, and invariably counterproductive for us to expect them to behave otherwise. Allowances must be made, outbursts gently overlooked, appearance taken with a grain of salt...within reason, of course. But churches that want all that enter their hallowed doors to get cleaned up in speech, dress, and actions *beforehand* should hardly be surprised by dust on the hymnals.

On the other hand, Christians who name the Name are *and should be* accountable to a higher standard. Sadly, it is not uncommon for God's people to let others down. Regularly. In both little ways and big. Solomon wrote that it is a "glory to overlook an offense" (Proverbs 19:11b), but it isn't easy!

1 How has your experience with Christians affected your definition of true Christianity? Do you have positive examples as well as negative ones?

_____

_____

_____

_____

_____

2 Is it easier or harder to forgive fellow believers when they hurt you than it is to forgive people in the world? Why?

_____

_____

_____

_____

_____

3 Why are we surprised when the world acts like the world? How does this affect our attitudes in society, the political arena, the entertainment industry?

_____

_____

_____

_____

_____

4   Statistically, the church ranks fairly equal to the world in terms of divorce, premarital sex, teen pregnancy, etc. What does this communicate to the world, and why?

_____

_____

_____

_____

_____

I feel your pain...

There may be some in the study group who have been so hurt by people within the church—or know people in such circumstances—that they have given up on attending altogether. I totally understand. As a teenager, I was molested by a trusted family friend in our church. Over the years, I've suffered from the gossip mill that routinely operates among congregations of all shapes and sizes. I've sought help and counsel from pastors and left wondering why I'd bothered. I know what it's like to have someone at church say, "I'll be there for you" and then disappear.

I know what it's like to have Christian friends forsake me based on rumor or assumption—or even based on *accurate* information…to walk into church and not feel safe, shadowing my husband David so that no one is able to catch me alone and inflict more pain. I know what it's like to watch people be publicly affirmed as pillars of the congregation who have *knowingly* hurt me and my loved ones. It was at just such a point during a Sunday morning service that David turned to me and said simply, "I think we need to be somewhere else."

Unfortunately, "somewhere else" can easily become *nowhere at all*. Once we get out of the habit of regular church attendance, myriad activities rush in to distract, take priority, and demand our time. Especially if you have been part of one church for a number of years, finding a new congregation can be extremely challenging. If the place you regarded as "family" didn't work out, how can a *new* place—filled with complete strangers—possibly be better?

If you fall into the category of "formerly churched," my prayer is that this study will encourage you to make the effort to step back into the fray. Strictly speaking, church attendance is an obedience issue not to be treated lightly (see Hebrews 10:25), but more than that, it's a "God thing." Church isn't full of perfect people, but it is full of people God wants us to learn to love. With all the potential for hurt in the church, you've got to admit it does make the perfect *classroom*!

5 Do you know someone who has "given up" on church, even on faith in God? Was he or she driven out by hurtfulness or did the exodus reflect personal struggles or conviction?

_____

_____

_____

_____

6 People often say things like "I can worship God just as well out on the golf course as in church"…but do they? Discuss expressions of worship mentioned in the Bible. Which ones are best suited to solitude, which to assemblies?

_____

_____

_____

_____

Where there's a will, there's a way...

Prior to going on the mission field, David and I attended a YWAM Discipleship Training School (DTS) in Lindale, Texas. During the three-month classroom phase, we absorbed the wit and wisdom of numerous gifted teachers from bases around the world as well as non-YWAMers in the ministry of equipping the saints.

You can well imagine that much of a *discipleship training* program dealt with that sticky command of Jesus to his *first* disciples: love one another. Interpersonal relationships are extremely important when living in community, as missionaries often do, since that fishbowl existence stands as a daily witness to the mission *field*. As one man put it, "Jesus has given you the ability to get along with every other person on the face of the planet." Communal living puts this precept to the test as none other I've experienced.

Paul said it like this: "For he himself is our peace, who has...destroyed the barrier, the dividing wall of hostility" (Ephesians 2:14). In other words, we have the God-given ability to recognize interpersonal problems and deal with them appropriately.

Another DTS teacher said, "You can get along with anyone if you're humble enough." In most cases, that's true. However, "getting along" isn't all God is after. He wants a spotless bride, remember, not a social group that has learned to put on a pretty face every Sunday morning.

7 Any cohesive group can substitute for church if obedience to Christ is subtracted from the equation. What groups can you think of that fill that need in your community? (ex. Scouts, community theater, etc.)

_____

_____

_____

_____

_____

8 Are the same problems that one might find at church there as well? What are the differences?

_____

_____

_____

_____

_____

9 Western missionaries are notorious for trying to export their cultural standards in addition to the gospel. What effect should Paul's words (from Ephesians 2:14 above) have on us when dealing with members of a different denomination, race, or nationality?

_____

_____

_____

_____

Please the Lord—*please.*

The *New American Standard Bible* version of Ephesians 5:10 tells us to "learn what is pleasing to the Lord." We may be better able to understand what pleases the Lord when we, first, look at things that do *not* please him. Then we are better able to turn them around. Take things up a notch, spiritually. Dig a little deeper.

The purpose of this study, then, is to acknowledge with excruciating honesty that (1) God's people regularly behave *baaadly* toward one another, (2) we should learn how to avoid such behavior in ourselves, and (3) we need to respond to the hurts and those who cause them according to godly principles.

So, in this workbook, we'll look at specific ways in which God's people let each other down. Many people have responded to my invitation and come forward with a willingness to share their stories (some of them with tears) and the hurts that still—perhaps after many years—trouble them. Some of the illustrations I use in this workbook are from my own life; some are (as far as I know) imaginary. And don't worry if you think you've recognized someone—names and details have been changed to protect the guilty.

Was it right to ask others…to ask this group…to look at so much negativity? It doesn't seem…*Nice* (an important character quality, especially in the South). And aren't we to "judge not"? Alas, Matthew 7:1 is one of the most misquoted verses in the Bible. As M. Scott Peck writes in *People of the Lie,* Jesus followed those words with the speck-and-beam analogy in which he taught how to help a brother overcome sin. "What he meant was that we should judge others only with great care, and that such carefulness begins with self-judgment."[3] That means that in some cases we'll be talking about the "*baaad* sheep" I've known or heard about. And in some cases, we'll be talking about *you*.

Reflection & Encouragement

Jesus commanded his disciples to love one another. He also sent them out into the world to preach the Gospel. Two millennia later, the Gospel has spread to far corners of the globe, but the shelves of Christian bookstores are still lined with challenges to love. Spreading the Good News will be much more effective as we learn to grasp that one essential point—to love. As I heard one minister say, "If you don't have it together at home, you've got nothing to export." As we look at our church "homes," let us commit to doing the work of "getting it together" there.

Closing Prayer

Heavenly Father, we have been hurt by your children. As your children, we have hurt others. Give us a sensitivity as we begin this study to see others through your eyes of love, to see situations from the perspective of your plans and purposes. We commit this study to you, in Jesus' precious name. Amen.

Week 1 Memory Verse

"'A new command I give you: Love one another. As I have loved you, so you must love one another. By this all men will know that you are my disciples, if you love one another.'"
—John 13:34-35

Homework

❶ Make a list this week of instances when Christians—true or so-called—let you down. Spend time in prayer lifting each person up. Then make a list of times you know that you let *others* down, and include those people in prayer as well.

❷ Do Week Two to prepare for next week.

Gossip & cliques

"Do not let any unwholesome talk come out of your mouths, but only what is helpful for building others up according to their needs, that it may benefit those who listen. And do not grieve the Holy Spirit of God..."

—*Ephesians 4:29-30a*

Foreword to Week 2

Not long ago, our women's Bible study got into a discussion of whether or not *all* gossip is sin. If you've been lying awake at night pondering this, let me put your mind at rest: yes. Yes, gossip is sin. Jesus never said a kind word about *unkind* words. Although there are times we are called to bring *strong* words, words that may initially hurt, they are to be spoken under special circumstances, out of love. To a person's face—never behind his back!

As believers, we know—because the Holy Spirit bears witness within us—that gossip is wrong. When we hear others gossiping, we're offended at some level to the degree that we have been trained to be sensitive to sin. When we observe gossip taking its toll on a congregation—especially if we are the subject—the temptation is just to bail. Instead, we're going to look at the root of gossip, talk about times we've been hurt by it (or hurt others) and discuss ways to rid it from the church.

Cliques go together with gossip like apple butter and bread—find a gossip, and you'll probably find a clique...and vice versa. While church is supposed to be a welcoming, inviting place, cliques ooze exclusivity and snobbery. And yes, there's sometimes a very fine line between long-established, intimate friendships and cliques. Newcomers, especially newcomers with emotional chips on their shoulders, can easily misinterpret the former positive and desirable entity with the latter *baaad* twin. That being the case, it's all the more important to de-clique de church (sorry).

Opening Prayer

Lord, we sometimes wonder why you put up with us at all. You clearly said that the world should recognize us as your followers by our love for one another. Instead, we are often guilty of not only being unloving in our hearts, but opening our mouths and giving voice to that un-love so that others are poisoned as well. Forgive us, teach us, open your Word and open our hearts that we may learn to truly reflect your love for others. In Jesus' precious name we pray, Amen.

The Worst Gossip was the first...

Years ago, as I alluded to in my prayer above, I allowed the gossip of someone else to poison me as well. My sister and I were settling into our seats at a school auditorium in anticipation of a musical performance when I spotted a familiar hair-do across the room. "Oh look," I nudged my sister. "Satan's sitting in the second row." It was a vengeful and completely unloving thing to say, I freely admit. At the time, wallowing in my hurt, it was my honest assessment.

The person I saw was someone who had, by her own admission, gossiped about me for *years*. Elisabeth George, in her book and study guide entitled *A Woman's High Calling*, points out that the word "slanderer" is derived from the Greek *diabolos*, a word used in the Bible 34 times to describe Satan![4] Had I been less focused on the hurt that person had caused me, I may have been able to look beyond her and recognize my true enemy, Satan, who had a hold on this woman.

1 Are you surprised that gossip (slander) ranks right up there with Evil Personified? Why or why not?

_____

_____

_____

_____

_____

2   Look at Proverbs 10:18-20, along with this week's memory verse, Ephesians 4:29-30a, to contrast the words of the wise and the words of the foolish. Have you ever heard a bit of gossip that sounded *wise*?

_____

_____

_____

_____

_____

3   Without using names, describe a time when you saw another person as the enemy.

_____

_____

_____

_____

_____

4   How would your actions or perspective have changed had you seen the real enemy, Satan, in the situation?

_____

_____

_____

_____

_____

Behind a Veil of Concern...

At an elegant reception, Linda was enjoying her plate of mints, sausage balls, and eggrolls when Sheila, with whom she attended church and had known since high school, approached her with a warm smile. They did the small talk routine for a few minutes before Sheila asked tentatively, "So how are you and Gene doing? Everything okay?"

"Yes," Linda frowned, her curiosity aroused. "Why do you ask?"

Sheila glanced away. "Well, I heard you were having problems—"

Linda forced herself to remain calm. She and Gene had emerged from a rough year. And although they hadn't tried to hide anything, their personal life (as far as they knew) hadn't been discussed outside the family or marriage counseling sessions. "Really. Who told you *that?*"

"Oh, I couldn't say," Sheila said virtuously.

Linda stared at the uneaten food on her plate, tears welling up. "Please tell your *friend* that Gene and I are just fine." And she walked away.

Locating Gene by the punch bowl, Linda whispered, "I'm ready to leave when you are," slipping an arm through his and kissing his cheek. *If the gossips are watching,* she thought, *maybe that will shut them up.*

And they're *always* watching, aren't they? Gossips keep a keen eye on what we wear, how close we stand to members of the opposite sex, how loudly we laugh, the number of months after a couple gets married that a pregnancy is announced, who asks for prayer and for what during Bible study.

5 Share a time you were the butt of gossip. How did it make you feel? Did you respond with a godly attitude, or in anger?

_____

_____

_____

_____

_____

6 How did it affect your relationship with the person (or group) who hurt you?

_____

_____

_____

_____

7 Because it encourages a slanderer to continue, *listening* to gossip is just as harmful as generating it in the first place. Was Sheila's sin as great or less than that of the source she refused to disclose?

_____

_____

_____

_____

8 What would have been a more loving response by Sheila when Linda's marriage came up in conversation with another person? Read Proverbs 16:28, 18:8, and 20:19 for ideas.

_____

_____

_____

_____

Baaad Things Come in Small Packages...

A man rather severely criticized me after his wife complained she'd seen me feed a male friend a bite of birthday cake from my own fork. I tried to make some dry comment about missing the particular verse of Scripture forbidding such a thing, but the damage was done. I was offended that she was so offended that she led her husband to take up an offense against me!

Small thing? Yes, but years of such small things erode the complexion of our relationships in the body of Christ. And from *her! A grown woman in mini-skirts...why, I heard she even wore a bikini to a youth group pool party. And she has the nerve...*

Gossip is like that. When it pits us against each other, the fall-out can be fatal—precisely why Satan loves it so much. Gossip may be one of the smallest weapons in his arsenal, but like a poison-tipped arrow, it's one of the deadliest. Perspective is important—gossip isn't as serious as, say, rape or incest—but ignoring the problem because it is small and "everyone does it" creates an unhealthy atmosphere at church, one that is completely counterproductive to the cause of Christ.

"We all need a place for our secrets to be held and respected," wrote Drs. Henry Cloud and John Townsend in their book *Safe People*.[5] Aside from family, the local church should be the safest place we can be, filled with people who, because of our shared relationship with the Lord, love us and extend mercy and compassion to us.

9 Do you feel safe right now? If there is any lingering question about the group's commitment to confidentiality, this would be an excellent time to bring up concerns.

_____

_____

_____

_____

_____

10 Look at Proverbs 11:13. Judas "betrayed" Jesus with a kiss; discuss a gossip's role as betrayer? How important is it to you to be known as a "trustworthy" person?

_____

_____

_____

_____

11 How could a problem with gossip affect a church's ability to reach the lost in its community?

_____

_____

_____

_____

_____

If You Can't Say Something Nice...

Catherine lunched occasionally with a friend and the friend's son, who happened to pastor a local church. Things he said in front of Catherine about his own congregation were appalling. The pastor's justification was that he never said anything about a person that he wouldn't repeat in that person's presence. Catherine wasn't impressed. She said, "Whether the other person would mind or not, it's none of my business."

* * * * *

Although we never became members at a particular church, I met with the pastor to discuss some questions. When I asked about counseling, he threw up his hands. "I'm a teacher, not a counselor. If you want counseling, I can direct you to some fine individuals."

"Can you keep your mouth shut?" I asked. It shocked him a bit, but then he nodded, understanding that sometimes we don't need *advice*, just the freedom to vent. We need a trusted friend who has earned a history, a reputation, for listening to information without repeating it to others...even to *his or her* trusted friends.

12 A good rule of thumb about discussing a personal matter is not to talk to anyone who is neither part of the problem nor the solution. Sometimes the solution may be to simply blow off steam and get on with life. When was the last time you followed this advice? The last time you failed to follow it?

_____

_____

_____

_____

13 Has venting to someone you *thought* was trustworthy ever backfired? What lessons were learned?

_____

_____

_____

_____

_____

Silent partner...

Think back to Linda's conversation with Sheila. Although just the two of them were there, a third person was very much involved—the person who (perhaps in the guise of loving concern) brought the subject of Linda and Gene's troubles to Sheila's attention. Gossips can easily hide their true motives in the church setting, because we need to understand a situation in order to effectively pray about it, right?

I must have missed that Scripture too.

No speculation about Linda and Gene would in any way maximize a person's ability to pray for them. Even when we know all the facts (a rare occasion, to be sure), we have, at best, a two-dimensional reality. Only God knows the end from the beginning, discerning the hearts of the people involved as well as their actions. He never requires our *intellect* in order to respond to our *intercession.*

The people who discussed Linda and Gene's problems...behind their backs...may have had good intentions (or at least convinced *themselves* that they did), but gossip can have a darker side. Sheila's "source" may have been embroiled in marital problems herself and wished to divert attention to someone else. She might have even held a grudge against Linda or Gene for some perceived hurt in the past, totally unrelated to the present circumstances. Perhaps she enjoyed the sense of superiority and spirituality that came when she shared "new" information with an avid listener. She may have even willingly and knowingly tried to inflict pain, a weed among the wheat (see Matthew 13:24-30).

14 Elizabeth George quotes Frank M. Garafda as saying "The difference between a smart man and a wise man is that a smart man knows what to say and a wise man knows whether to say it or not."[6] How does that apply here? Do you provide more information than is necessary when asking others to pray for a friend, family member, or situation?

_____

_____

_____

_____

_____

15 Read James' passage on the potential hurtfulness caused by speech (3:1-12). Look closely at verse 10. How does the idea of "blessing and cursing" come into play with gossipy "prayer concerns"?

_____

_____

_____

_____

_____

16 Proverbs 18:21a says "The tongue has the power of life and death." Consider James' use of the saltwater and fresh water analogy above. Does saltwater promote life or death? Have you ever heard someone say a derogatory thing about a brother or sister and turn right around and say something "spiritual"?

_____

_____

_____

_____

_____

_____

Dealing head-on...

A juicy rumor spread throughout a church. Apparently a strange woman had taken up residence at the parsonage the day after the pastor's wife left town unexpectedly. Rather than let gossip destroy his ministry, the pastor took a proactive approach. The Sunday following his knowledge of the rumor, he directed the deacons to lock all exterior doors and stand guard at each one.

From the pulpit, he explained gently but firmly that his wife had been called away suddenly when her mother fell ill. "Knowing that I depend on my wife for so much, my sister—on her first visit to this friendly town—arrived to help. Someone turned a wholesome situation into a sordid rumor. I want to know who it was."

He paused. "We are not leaving this building until the person who started the rumor comes forward."

Aside from perhaps breaking a few fire marshal rules for safe assembly, I'd say that there was a minister who didn't fool around…with other women or with sin in the camp. Following a protracted, uneasy silence, the guilty party finally broke down in repentance. Unity was restored and God was glorified.

17 Why does gossip titillate? What draws us to it?

_____

_____

_____

_____

_____

18 Alice Roosevelt Longworth had the following motto embroidered on a cushion: "If you haven't got anything nice to say about anybody, come sit next to me."[7] Gossip gives us the ability to feel superior to others without them knowing it, a "vice enjoyed vicariously."[8] How do these attitudes compare with Jesus' teachings?

_____

_____

_____

_____

_____

19 Discuss familiar sayings about gossip such as "If you can't say something nice, don't say anything at all," "Sticks and stones may break my bones but names can never hurt me," etc. How effective are they at stopping gossip?

_____

_____

_____

_____

_____

A friendly rebuke...

Melanie sat across from Jane's kitchen table as they worked on a Sunday School project together. "I used to be close to Tammy," Jane confided wistfully, "until she and Eloise became friends and I got left out of the loop. I feel like they're always talking about me behind my back." She reached for a tissue to wipe her eyes. "I almost left the church because of it."

Melanie knew her friend needed to vent, but her heart sank. "Have you talked to them about it?"

"I tried, but they deny there's a problem."

"Let's pray about it," Melanie said. The women asked God to bless Tammy and Eloise, to minister to their deepest needs and hurts, and to forgive them for hurting Jane. "Teach me to love my enemies...even when they're my friends," Jane wept quietly.

Within a few days, Tammy stopped by and began criticizing Eloise.

"You know what?" said Jane. "You've known me a long time, and you know that I'm capable of much worse than anything Eloise did. My sin nailed Jesus to the cross. *Your* sin nailed Jesus to the cross. Let's talk about that, instead of Eloise. If you need to go straighten this out, I'd be glad to join you. Otherwise, let's change the subject."

At first, Tammy was offended. She got up to leave, but abruptly stopped at the door. "You're right. I've been a terrible friend. To Eloise, to you, to the Lord."

20 Read Ephesians 4:29-32. How does the passage relate to gossip?

_____

_____

_____

_____

_____

Unity Builder

If gossip has wreaked havoc on members of your group (and even if it hasn't!), consider scheduling a time of affirmation to combat the damage. Pray about something positive and creative to say about each person. For instance, one leader prayed about a specific flower with which to describe each woman in her small group. (Over 20 years later, white roses are still my favorite because of what that lovely woman said...though it was likely the rose's *thorniness* that gave her the idea.)

Point and clique...

Rosa had attended the church for several months and looked forward to being a part of the music ministry. It wasn't just that the group was talented; they worked together like a well-oiled machine, having a lot of fun in the process.

After a few weeks of attending practices and joining the team on the platform for services, however, she announced to Freda, one of the other singers, that she didn't think it was for her. "Cliques just aren't my cup of tea," Rosa sniffed. "I put forth as much time and effort as anyone, but I don't feel nearly as welcome."

Freda's face clouded over. "I know everyone's pleased you joined us. You just need to understand that many of us have been doing this—with each other!—for a decade. We know each other so well we finish each other's sentences. We've invested years into our relationships. Surely you don't think it's going to be the same for you—you just started coming here!"

Rosa's face reddened. "I guess I never looked at it that way."

21 Christians can be guilty of spiritual fornication—they want the benefits of relationship, with none of the responsibilities of commitment. Rosa wanted instant buddies—discuss similar situations you have experienced.

_____

_____

_____

_____

_____

22 Look at 1 Corinthians 1:10-12. Paul called the Corinthian problem "division," but it's got "clique" written all over it. Churches often unwittingly foster such problems by segregating ministries. What are some ways this can be avoided? (E.g. rotating Sunday school teachers every other month so teachers can fellowship in peer-level classes, having the youth participate in kids' and adults' events periodically, etc.)

_____

_____

_____

_____

_____

Reflection & Encouragement

Gossip is anti-Christian, unloving, troublesome, and divisive. Solomon wrote that "the words of a gossip are like choice morsels" (Proverbs 18:8), but they should taste bitter on our lips, reminding us to go no further. And it doesn't really matter if the gossip is true or false. Paul's guidelines for our thoughts (which yield words and actions) in Philippians 4:18 go beyond validity: "Finally, brothers, whatever is true, whatever is noble, whatever is right, whatever is pure, whatever is lovely, whatever is admirable—if anything is excellent or praiseworthy—think about such things."

Baaad sheep who gossip tend to stick like glue to those who will listen and provide fresh morsels for their personal entertainment—thus, cliques are born. Their words and behavior can do nothing *but* hurt.

Closing Prayer

Father, we invite you to convict us of times when we have sinned against brothers or sisters with gossip. Forgive us and "set a guard over [our mouths], O Lord; keep watch over the door of [our] lips" as David prayed in Psalm 141. Where we have listened to gossip, forgive us. Give us the courage to stand up for those who are not present to defend themselves. And where we have been hurt by gossip, help us to forgive. In Jesus' name, Amen.

Week 2 Memory Verse

"Do not let any unwholesome talk come out of your mouths, but only what is helpful for building others up according to their needs, that it may benefit those who listen. And do not grieve the Holy Spirit of God…"

—Ephesians 4:29-30a

Homework

❶ Is there a large-scale problem with gossip at your church? Have you personally been affected strongly by gossip and slander? As a group or individually, consider fasting one day this week, standing in prayer against this "blemish" on the bride of Christ. Pray for the conviction of the Holy Spirit to prepare the hearts of guilty parties for possible confrontation. Pray for a spirit of forgiveness for those who have been hurt. And pray, always, for the Lord to turn his light onto *your* heart as well.

❷ Do Week Three to prepare for next week.

Division—not just a math problem

"The faith which you have, have as your own conviction before God. Happy is he who does not condemn himself in what he approves."

—Romans 14:22, NASB

Foreword to Week 3

Now that we have a better understanding of the damage gossip can do, we move on to one of the things gossips gossip *about*—disputable matters. Quicker than you can say "contemporary music," *baaad* sheep can use these issues to cause division in a church, and between churches.

In elementary school, we used a mnemonic device to remember the order of functions for long division: <u>d</u>ad (divide), <u>m</u>om (multiply), <u>s</u>ister (subtract), <u>b</u>rother (bring down). Too bad there's not a similar device for dealing with division in the church. While God saw fit to give specific instructions about some things—the core of our belief system, the foundation of our behavior and ethics—he was surprisingly silent on a multitude of others.

Disputable matters can, if allowed, become festering thorns in a church's side. How loudly should worship music be played? Is too much lipstick immodest? Should we have Sunday evening services? Is it acceptable for members to smoke? Is blue carpet best for the sanctuary, or mauve? It is amazing how such things take on a life of their own, growing into high walls between us.

On a larger scale are the divisions between congregations. There is division among denominations about whether or not you can lose your salvation, division over whether or not it's appropriate to speak in tongues, and division over whether or not missions should be a church's primary focus.

The body of Christ is called to unity, and divisive people let us down. Jesus will return for a spotless, unified bride, and therefore, divisiveness is almost always counterproductive and offensive. There are exceptions, but we need to *recognize* division before we discern its specific nature.

Opening Prayer

Lord, you broke down the dividing wall between us by your death on the cross. Bring insight into ways that Satan is trying to rebuild obstacles to unity, ways he divides believer from believer, church from church, denomination from denomination. Unite us in your Holy Spirit, we ask in Jesus' name, Amen.

Addition Brings Division

Jesus said he came to fulfill the Law and the Prophets, not abolish them (Matthew 5:17). Note that he didn't come to add to the Law, either. At least in the case of John's Revelation, there is this dire warning: "If anyone adds anything to [the words of the prophecy], God will add to him the plagues described in this book" (22:18).

There are over 600 actual and implied laws in the Torah (the first five books of the Bible, attributed to Moses' authorship). Fortunately for Christians, most of whom are Gentiles (non-Jewish descent), the early church leaders took pity. When asked what laws Gentile converts should follow, the Council of Jerusalem sent out a memo: "It seemed good to the Holy Spirit and to us not to burden you with anything beyond the following requirements: You are to abstain from food sacrificed to idols, from blood, from the meat of strangled animals and from sexual immorality. You will do well to avoid these things" (Acts 15:28-29).

When we worked with YWAM, we didn't agree with every rule, but we obeyed them—we joined them, after all, not the other way around. Later, as a denominational schoolteacher, I ran into more rules in my contract: No smoking, drinking, dancing, R-rated movies, etc. (At the time, I was a member of a worship dance/Israeli folk dance troupe and returned my signed contract with a few stipulations—the next year, the contract read "no secular dancing.")

One day I remembered suddenly that I had violated the contract with nary a thought. At a wedding I'd attended some weeks earlier, we'd drunk a champagne toast. Worse, I'd danced with David! Eager to do the right thing, I stepped into the principal's office—for all I knew, he'd dock my pay.

Instead, he chuckled. "We're a little hypocritical when you think about it—love figure skating, hate dancing. What's really the difference?" When another official joined us, I repeated the particulars. Frowning, she asked if there were any students present.

"Other than my own kids, just Isaac," I said, unable to stop myself. "But I think I could buy him off."

When people feel strongly about such things, the "dance" between them, so to speak, can be an uneasy one without humility. My years at the school were a learning experience—for both sides, I think. They knew my non-denominational, charismatic background; I knew where they stood on upbeat music and displaying certain gifts of the spirit. We chose to "agree to disagree" without there being a problem relating. The only trouble I got into was for reading out of a non-King James Version Bible to my students and for washing the feet of fellow teachers.

1 What have you been asked to refrain from that wasn't, evidently, a problem for the original church?

_____

_____

_____

_____

_____

2 The principal's ability to laugh a little at the quirks of fundamentalism reveals the knowledge that they were not based on God's Word, but on man's preference. What rules have you encountered that fell into the same category?

_____

_____

_____

_____

_____

3 If the school had maintained that all dancing is sinful, I could not have remained with the dance ministry team and taught there too. Have you had to choose between two groups because of the rules of one of them? How did you make the choice?

_____

_____

_____

_____

_____

Division can bring multiplication...

Division isn't necessarily negative, of course. If a church embraces gross error, it would be wise to leave. When a small group grows to the point that intimacy among its members is impossible, it may be more productive to split into several small groups. The non-traditional Baptist church I attend was planted by a traditional congregation that saw a need in the community. The division with the new venture provided opportunity for growth among the two different entities. There wouldn't even be Protestant churches had Martin Luther not "split" from Catholicism.

There may be times when it's wise to seek a new church. Maybe it's because of lifelessness in the particular church or denomination. Maybe because of the church's resistance to spiritual obedience. Maybe for lack of support from the church leaders in bringing health and healing to the congregation. As my husband put it, "There are some hurts in life you can't avoid. Others you can."

The division we want to avoid is the nit picking, "us vs. them" mentality that arises when disputable matters take our eyes off real issues. In Scripture, Martha became indignant because her sister didn't help set the table. Meanwhile, her sister was listening while the Son of God was teaching in the living room. Mary was resolved on the "one thing", whereas Martha had an "us vs. them" perspective. Jesus rebuked Martha, albeit gently, urging her to maintain focus: "You are worried and upset about many things, but only one thing is needed" (Luke 10:41b-42).

4 Not every conflict can be resolved to everyone's satisfaction; not every division is the result of a conflict. Have you experienced a positive example of division? How did the change increase spiritual growth?

_____

_____

_____

_____

_____

5 Jesus, visiting Martha's home for only a short time, said her sister Mary "chose what is better" by sitting at his feet listening (Luke 10:39,42). How does that apply to our relatively brief hours spent at church and what we are focused on while there?

_____

_____

_____

_____

_____

A time to speak...

Amy was troubled by the church's requirements for leadership—actually only one point—the "agreement to total abstinence from alcohol." After spending time in study and prayer, she wrote what she hoped was a humble, balanced letter to the pastor and elders asking them to reconsider. Their outreach was to the unchurched segment of the community, the very people likely to perceive the requirement as an attempt to legislate private behavior. She speculated that since the Bible (hence, God) did not specifically forbid alcohol (rather, the sin of drunkenness), the requirement was questionable.

The response was favorable. "It's something we need to address," said one elder who called Amy to thank her. The pastor invited Amy to meet with the elders to discuss the matter further.

6   Do you feel strongly about a current church rule that you
believe to be potentially counterproductive to the cause
of Christ?

_____

_____

_____

_____

_____

7   Is there any scriptural basis for either the rule or your
opinion, or both?

_____

_____

_____

_____

_____

8   Have you complained (gossiped) about the matter, or
prayed for an opportunity to make an appeal?

_____

_____

_____

_____

_____

What's good for the goose...

While living at the YWAM training base, we ate pretty
well at the ccafeteria. One of the other mothers with young
children, however, was distressed at the amount of sugar in
the diet. During a small group discussion, she brought up the
fact that she had always kept her family on a very strict program in the past. Opinions were so strong you would have
thought we were arguing about meat sacrificed to idols!

It's just human nature for us to take a lesson we believe
God (or common sense) is teaching us, and run with it, con-

vinced that everyone we encounter would benefit as well. The mom didn't want her children eating sweets…fine. Wise, in fact. But one mother's preference should not an organization's rule make (thankfully, as I need chocolate).

Everyone goes through phases—listen exclusively to Christian music, stop reading anything but the Bible, give up television. There is nothing wrong with these periods of discipline; they can, in fact, accomplish much in our growth and development as Christians—as long as we understand that they are intended for our growth alone.

God told Jim to stop watching television because it took too much time out of his day. Great…for Jim. Casey felt the Lord prompt her to stop using make-up due to self-esteem issues. Wonderful…for Casey. No one else needs to agree with, or even know about, such personal changes.

9 When Casey stopped wearing make-up, her friend Lora was offended, assuming that Casey now considered make-up to be sinful. By extension, since Lora wore make-up, she further assumed Casey regarded her as sinful. Have you ever walked through a discipline that made others uncomfortable?

_____

_____

_____

_____

_____

10 Have you ever felt "put off" or "put down" by something another person felt called by God to do?

_____

_____

_____

_____

_____

11 I once stopped shaving my legs as a time- and money-saving exercise. After two weeks, my husband informed me that he'd received a word from the Lord—I was to start shaving again. Immediately! Discuss other instances when a person's decision to make a behavioral change could have a negative (!) impact on others.

_____

_____

_____

_____

_____

When I was your age...

Craig takes his responsibilities as a deacon seriously. He admits to being frustrated, however, by the steady stream of complaints from some of the older members of the congregation. "You know the drill...'back in my day,' one will start, 'we never sang that kind of music/paid for puppets to entertain the kids/used blue paint, etc.'" Most of them served as deacons themselves at one time or another, but Craig struggles with all the armchair quarterbacking. "I just wish they'd give us credit for doing what we think is best."

* * * * *

Sylvia is a children's ministry leader, a veritable fireball eager to implement new ideas and strategies to reach the children of her community and congregation with the Gospel. "Every time I make the slightest change, I get flak. 'Why didn't you leave it the way it was?' 'So-and-so never did it that way!' Sheesh—sometimes I wish So-and-so was still in charge!"

* * * * *

You've probably heard the story about the woman who cut the ends off the roast before putting the pan in the oven. When asked why, she replied that it was the way her mother had done it. Her mother, watching, said that was how her mother had done it. When Grandma was consulted, she said her pan was too small for the roast!

It's easy to get into a rut, doing things a certain way out of habit rather than need. When criticism comes over disputable matters, we should examine the matter. Why are we doing it that way? Paul instructed us to "make every effort to do what leads to peace and to mutual edification" (Romans 14:19). Sometimes, there is a valid need to change or even—because a brother or sister is offended—no valid reason not to change.

If the reasoning is sound, however, there are four important words to remember about criticism: It doesn't really matter. Aunt Bea disagrees with your choice of solo? You sang it as unto the Lord. Deacon Joe thinks country music is of the devil and your favorite artist is George Strait? He doesn't have to listen to it, and you don't have to play it when he's in the car (more likely, the truck).

Division over disputable matters may involve trivialities, but the warning against it is anything but trivial: "But avoid foolish controversies and…quarrels about the law, because these are unprofitable and useless. Warn a divisive person once, and then warn him a second time. After that, have nothing to do with him. You may be sure that such a man is warped and sinful; he is self-condemned" (Titus 3:9-11).

Yikes!

12 Have you experienced resistance to a new idea within the church? How was it handled? Were feelings hurt, or was fellowship helped?

_____

_____

_____

_____

_____

Reflection & Encouragement

Like the poor, there will always be disputable matters among us. God didn't address every possible issue in his Word, so we are left to prayer—and sometimes to just hashing it out. As Mark Twain once said, however, "It ain't those parts of the Bible that I can't understand that bother me; it is the parts that I do understand." If our focus is on obedience to what God did say, we'll have far less time to get into trouble arguing the issues about which he said nothing.

I have a feeling there are a great many things we consider to be quite important that the creator of the universe cares little about indeed.

Closing Prayer

Gracious Father, we behave like unruly children so much of the time, wasting time and energy arguing with one another over things which, in the eternal scope of things, amount to only so much as dust. Forgive us, and show us how to focus on the truly important things—the things on your heart and mind. When we have to address disputable matters, give us an attitude of humility so that they do not bring division in the body of Christ. In his name, Amen.

Week 3 Memory Verse

"The faith which you have, have as your own conviction before God. Happy is he who does not condemn himself in what he approves."

—Romans 14:22, NASB

Homework

❶ In your experience, what builds church unity? Make a list, writing down corresponding Scriptures (if possible).

❷ If you know someone who has recently left your church, send a note or make a phone call just to remind that person you're thinking of him or her, and praying for God's best.

❸ Do Week Four to prepare for next week.

Control freaks & other master manipulators

"...I urge you, brothers, in view of God's mercy, to offer your bodies as living sacrifices, holy and pleasing to God — this is your spiritual act of worship. ...Do not think of yourself more highly than you ought"

—Romans 12:1,3

Foreword to Week 4

There is something within us that fights to maintain control, and it isn't completely due to the sin nature with which we are born. God bestows on each person a free will, as sovereign as the law of gravity and about as likely to be divinely overruled. It's an amazing thing, really — the King of Kings and Lord of Lords, who must restrain his own power so a simple "hello" doesn't blow me to smithereens, bows to *my* will and waits patiently for me to submit. He never manipulates, pulls on heartstrings, pushes, prods, or deceives in order to get me to come around to his way of doing it.

For that very reason, Paul urged us to *offer ourselves* to God. If we don't come freely, there's no point in coming at all, but the problem with living sacrifices is that we keep crawling down off the altar! We want to live for God. Then we don't. Then we do. Then we don't. And still the Lord waits patiently.

His people, on the other hand, our fellow "living sacrifices" who fill sanctuaries each Sunday morning and Wednesday night, often seem to have no qualms at all about trying to control others. Many people, to a certain extent, fall into what Carmen Renee Berry calls the "Messiah Trap" in her book *When Helping You Is Hurting Me.*[9] We want something done, it depends on us to get it done, and therefore it doesn't matter who we have to step on/manipulate/control in order to make it happen.

Because churches are generally leaders in the community, they are a natural draw for people who, whether consciously or not, seek positions of control. Think about our vocabulary: lord, serve, worship, submit, obey, commandments. For those with a weakness in this area, it is easy to lose sight of *whom* we are to obey—"God, rather than men" (Acts 5:29b).

Baaad sheep that control and manipulate are a *major* let-down because they make us feel used and taken advantage of. Dealing with them requires energy better used elsewhere. Our response to "control freaks" also requires that we take a look at our own hearts—why do we let others control us? Why can manipulators make us feel guilty? The Lord wants us to recognize control freaks—not only to help us avoid their manipulation, but also to deal with issues in our own lives that set us up as targets.

Opening Prayer

Holy Father, you set the universe in motion and set our minds at ease. You command the winds and seas and yet wait for us to approach your throne. When we consider your greatness we are humbled, but too quickly we return to delusions of grandeur. Teach us to rule ourselves correctly so that we don't try to rule others. In Jesus' name we ask this, Amen.

It all depends on me...

Harvey has been the choir director of his church for as long as anyone can remember. Talented in both music and administrative skills, he nevertheless refuses to call out the page numbers of the hymns he's leading. "Everybody knows this song," he'll say and off they go, members scrambling to find the index and visitors left out of the loop altogether.

Harvey would never think of himself as a control freak, but for a few isolated moments in church each week, when the congregation is trying to literally get on the same page as he is, he subconsciously relishes his power over them.

* * * * *

Jayne's controlling tendencies are more subtle. When a women's group from another denomination—one known to be somewhat narrow in its spiritual focus—invited her to share at their monthly meeting, she was thrilled at the prospect of enlightening her sisters in the Lord with some of the truths she'd learned over the years.

Instead, the message went over like the proverbial lead balloon. Sensing the anointing of the Holy Spirit, Jayne shared and shared and…the women sat, expressionless. Returning home, she flung herself across her bed and sobbed, "I blew it! The chance of a lifetime to reach those women and I blew it!"

In the ensuing silence she recognized the still, small voice of the Lord speaking to her heart. "What makes you think you're important enough to fail?" Suddenly she realized that, except for the issue of personal obedience, what she did or didn't say was of relatively small consequence. God was still God. His truth would reach those who sought it, regardless of appearances to the contrary, regardless of who, ultimately, brought that truth. She wouldn't have taken credit for "success," and she wasn't responsible for what looked to be "failure." *She was not in control.*

1 Paul warned us not to "think of ourselves more highly than we ought." What does Harvey's stubbornness communicate to others?

_____

_____

_____

_____

_____

2 How did Jayne's sense of self-importance set her up for a feeling of failure?

_____

_____

_____

_____

_____

3 Have you ever been sure things would go one way, only to feel as if the result was an utter failure? Was it, from heaven's vantagepoint?

_____

_____

_____

_____

_____

The Gospel According to Hollywood...

If you rooted for the main characters in the film *Butch Cassidy and the Sundance Kid*, you were manipulated. If you wanted Francesca to find true happiness with Robert (*The Bridges of Madison County*), you were manipulated. If you were sorry when Harrison Ford drove away from the Amish farmhouse in the movie *Witness*, you were manipulated.

Hollywood is the Master Manipulator. The entertainment industry works hard to convince otherwise thinking people that it knows what's best. Butch and Sundance were thieves, yes, but their handsome quirkiness gave them the right to steal. Francesca's passionless husband didn't appreciate her; therefore, he didn't deserve her. Harrison Ford's solo exit from Amish country and the woman who stayed behind was a rare incidence of a movie character doing the right thing.

Hollywood tugs at our emotions, giving us only a small piece of the puzzle on which to base opinions. Manipulators in the church can be guilty of the same things.

* * * * *

Carl was the pastor of a small church. From outward appearance, it must have seemed odd that the congregation did not grow by leaps and bounds—he was a charismatic leader, knowledgeable in the Word, adept at teaching. What was not readily evident was that *Carl* didn't want the church to grow.

You see, even a talented man like Carl could only control so many people at one time. His perspective—his voiced perspective—would have been that a good shepherd can only care for so many sheep, but his "sheep" would eventually reach a different conclusion.

* * * * *

Some churches tend to put a strong emphasis on submission to pastoral authority as pastors thrust themselves into the most personal details of their parishioners' lives. The result becomes a perfect climate in which the weeds of manipulation and control can flourish.

Emily was a teenager in one of these churches, eagerly seeking a deeper walk with God. Her church embraced the stance toward (forced) submission, and although she believes the leadership sincerely believed God was speaking through the teaching, their sincerity didn't prevent matters from getting out of hand.

People asked the pastor for advice on everything from whom to marry to how many bathrooms to put in their new home. Visitors sometimes eerily felt they were witnessing a cult, but those on the inside were too deep in deception to see it for themselves.

The fact that the individual faith of most members did not shipwreck on the rocky coastline of the manipulation is a testimony to God's grace. He honored seeking hearts and ultimately protected them—and does so in churches all across the country—but pastoral manipulation often leaves behind a wake of heartache and abuse, as we will see when we meet Emily again in Session Eight.

4   Bill Cassada, in an essay entitled "God of the Heart...Church of the Mind," points out that the healthy servant leadership spoken of in the Bible has given way to an unhealthy hierarchical system.[10] Discuss Matthew 20:25-27 in this context.

_____

_____

_____

_____

_____

5   When it comes to submission, people can easily go too far in the opposite direction, acting as if *submission* is a dirty word, but read Ephesians 5:21 and Hebrews 13:17. To whom must leaders (in the church, home, government, etc.) ultimately "give an account"?

_____

_____

_____

_____

If I don't do it, it won't get done...

Sarah leads the children's church ministry and is regularly exhausted. When asked about the possibility of delegating more duties to give her some free time, Sarah laughed. "I could, but then I'd have to take my hands off. I'm too much of a control freak to do that!"

Author Berry says "Messiahs" believe two things: If they don't do it (whatever "it" may be), no one will—or if others do "it", they won't do it properly. Sounding almost contradictory is the second idea—the personal needs of the "Messiah" don't matter. Sarah could get help with many of her projects, but wants them done "right." She is (perhaps subconsciously) convinced that her need for less stress isn't as important as her ministry.

* * * * *

Tony suggested the church launch a newsletter. "Why don't you do it?" the pastor replied, making resources available for printing and distribution. Everything went well until the newsletter included a particular short article by Tony. The pastor was concerned that people had been offended. "They're wondering why *you're* teaching them."

When pressed, however, the pastor admitted that not a single person had complained. In fact, comments had been unanimously favorable! Only the pastor was offended—Tony's opinion in the article differed from his own.

6   "Messiahs" often end up in leadership positions in the church and community because, on the surface, they want to make a difference and help others. How could a pastor, for instance, exert control disguised as caring?

_____

_____

_____

_____

_____

7   Tony's pastor fit Berry's "Messiah" mold by assuming that (1) he needed to do the teaching or it would not be done *properly* and (2) congregational needs for his (right)

opinion outweighed his need to delegate the newsletter to Tony. Have you come into contact with someone who fit the mold differently?

_____

_____

_____

_____

_____

You are so special...

When area newcomers Bob and Delores opened the church door (with no small amount of fear and trembling), the love and acceptance they found inside overwhelmed them. A year later, they told a different story. "If you're well-dressed, they go all out, but we've seen others practically snubbed. And when I asked for a financial report, you'd have thought I had four heads!"

They couldn't put their fingers on any one glaring example, but realized that they hadn't really grown spiritually over the previous year. There was scant interaction with other congregations; missions work was not discussed. There was also a large turnover—families that stayed tended to look and act much the same. "We left with a bad taste in our mouths."

8   It can be as hard to leave an unhealthy church as it is to leave an unhealthy relationship. Better, by far, to avoid being ensnared in the first place. One essay suggests the following "red flags" to watch out for: "love-bombing" visitors with too much attention and flattery, a lack of healthy debate on non-essential issues, emphasis on performance (such as everyone using a particular translation of the Bible) and/or a personality (usually the pastor), a history of disgruntled members and/or staff, "pet" Scriptures and/or sayings, secrecy, elitism ("We're the only ones with the complete truth"), isolationism, and a "gut feeling" that something is wrong.[11] Have you heard of, or experienced, any of these with a Christian organization or church?

_____

_____

_____

_____

_____

My way or the highway...

Dennis and Marie volunteered to help with the new contemporary service on their military base. Before long, the fledgling congregation sensed something was wrong. The senior chaplain constantly worked to drive wedges between it and the traditional congregation, which he personally led. When the contemporary service grew larger than that one, he announced that it must meet at a much less convenient location and time.

"It was a deliberate slap in the face. He also withheld designated funds from us," Marie says. "When a meeting was called to resolve the conflicts, the chaplain blatantly lied about things Dennis had spoken to him previously about. I couldn't believe it! But I just sat there and said nothing—he was the pastor."

The most negatively affected people were members of the contemporary service's children's ministry, already putting in many hours of weekly preparation. "There were such bitterness and hard feelings, it really stunted our growth spiritually. Some people just left, but the tension in the rest of us was obvious. I'm not even sure the man was *saved*."

9 Paul wrote to the church at Corinth that their "meetings (did) more harm than good" (1 Corinthians 11:17). He was speaking to a specific problem surrounding the Lord's Supper, but his words apply to Dennis and Marie's story. Have you heard someone use the pulpit to promote a private agenda?

_____

_____

_____

_____

10 Marie and Dennis saw the situation from a different perspective than the chaplain, but their individual perspectives differed as well, with Dennis being more concerned with giving the chaplain the benefit of the doubt. How might control and manipulations within a church drive wedges within relationships as well?

_____

_____

_____

_____

_____

Do as I do...

A speaker visiting a church that had survived its initial involvement with manipulation, only to experience continued unrest, sought the Lord for insight. "There is a crack in the foundation," he told the congregation, "and it starts at the top." Leaders, while successfully guiding the group through a rough transition from a loose-knit pastor-controlled fellowship to a more cohesive pastor-served church, still retained seeds of error. God was calling them to repentance. Fortunately, they received the word of correction.

We *all* must stay soft and humbled to the correction of the Holy Spirit; he will faithfully reveal any desires to control others. Leaders, however, are held to a higher standard. In a very real way, they represent the Lord "who being in very nature God, did not consider equality with God something to be grasped, but made himself nothing, taking the very nature of a servant…" (Philippians 2:6-7a).

Despite the heightened degree of accountability, however, leaders are first and foremost human beings…*fallen* human beings, at that. They must be especially careful, then, that they do not misuse their positions of authority in the church.

11 From where does the idea originate that admitting one's faults is a sign of weakness?

_____

_____

_____

12 Are Christian leaders who publicly confess error likely to increase or decrease their credibility? Discuss the much-publicized cases of televangelists such as Jim Bakker and Jimmy Swaggart.

_____

_____

_____

_____

_____

The buck stops here...

Jack was a well-liked teacher and club sponsor at a Christian school. He was also an ordained minister. The pastor over the school, however, informed him that he was no longer considered "qualified" to teach Bible, even though the man had never observed Jack in the classroom setting. Shattered, Jack was denied a request for a school board review, considered suing the school for breach of contract, and left the school.

* * * * *

Jenny needed to discuss a conflict with a church member who invited the pastor to sit in. Jenny didn't understand why, but having already counseled with the associate pastor, she asked him to join in as *her* support. When she arrived, the associate pastor's absence was conspicuous. "I couldn't tie up the entire staff with this," the pastor curtly told her, even though the meeting was after office hours.

"The reasons for all this became obvious when we started talking," Jenny says. "The pastor had instigated the problem with the other member and didn't want anyone else to know it! He cautioned us to 'keep the matter within this room.' Well, duh! Otherwise, *everyone* would find out what a mess he caused."

Jenny's trust of the pastor was damaged more by his *handling* of the matter than his original actions. She was hurt even more by the associate pastor's failure to follow through. "He said he'd be there. What kind of 'brother' is that?" God worked through the situation, however. Jenny had a history of compliance. "I'm cured now. I'll never blindly obey leadership and assume they know it all. Ever."

* * * * *

John was an elder with a long-standing reputation for loyal service. When the pastor asked for opinions on a pet project, John raised a few concerns. The next week, he received a letter from the pastor. "I trust you and your family will be able to find another church that will be more suited to your needs."

"Since when do pastors tell people to leave?!" John's wife said. "He *asked* for opinions!" She was so flabbergasted by his actions that she wanted to stop going to church altogether. Although they're still seeking the Lord as to possible steps of actions with the former church's governing body, they *have,* fortunately, found another church home.

13 Have you been asked to take a stand against a recognized authority? Did you hesitate to "touch my anointed ones" (Psalm 105:15)? Read the entire psalm; who actually *were* the "anointed ones" to which the psalmist referred?

_____

_____

_____

_____

_____

14 Should Jack have pursued the matter with the school board or through litigation? Why or why not?

_____

_____

_____

_____

_____

15 *Natural* submissiveness and compliance sometimes runs counter to *spiritual* submissiveness. Can you relate to Jenny's experience and response?

_____

_____

_____

_____

16 What would you do in John's case? Let it ride, announce it at church, write a letter of complaint, request a meeting?

_____

_____

_____

_____

Reflection & Encouragement

The ability to recognize manipulation will help us avoid much pain and frustration, but it is also important to recognize controlling tendencies within ourselves. We must, by a conscious act of our wills, remain on the altar of sacrifice daily, hourly. Only then will we not be sucked into the world's way of "lording over."

The desire to control others is a result of the Fall. When Adam and Eve rebelled against God, he pointed out that thereafter, Eve would desire (literally, "desire to control") Adam, but that Adam would still exercise control over her. Cain controlled Abel's actions by killing him. Nations wage war to control other nations. We live in a world where multiple systems control various aspects of our daily lives.

Conversely, church is to be a safe haven, a place where Christians serve one another in different capacities, no one "better" or "higher" than others, but fulfilling individual ministries so that the entire body of Christ is built up. Manipulators and control freaks have no place within church walls...unless they've come to repent.

Closing Prayer

Lord, you came to serve and call *us* to serve. Forgive us for using others to get our own way, for building ourselves up for selfish motives. Help us to recognize even the slightest manipulation in our words and deeds and body language. Forgive us when we fail. Help us to see as you see, serve as you serve, love as you love. In Jesus' name, we thank you. Amen.

Week 4 Memory Verse

"...I urge you, brothers, in view of God's mercy, to offer your bodies as living sacrifices, holy and pleasing to God—this is your spiritual act of worship. ...Do not think of yourself more highly than you ought"

—*Romans 12:1,3*

Homework

❶ Make a list of external controls in your life. Examples might include the time clock at work, your child's gymnastic lessons, speed limit signs, government, the show you simply *have* to watch each night (or record on TiVo©!). Which ones did God place there? Which did you invite? Are there any you need to avoid?

_____

_____

_____

_____

_____

❷ Paul instructed us to pray for our leaders (1 Timothy 2:2). As you pray, consider the heightened temptation leaders have for manipulation and ungodly control and ask God's protection on them.

❸ Do Week Five to prepare for next week.

Peace with God

Our family of six lived in India for most of 1987 working with Youth With A Mission (YWAM). While there, a national told us that there were three religious groups in his country, each one with its own reputation. "The Muslims are known for their lust; the Hindus, their deception. And Christians," he said sadly, "are known for stabbing each other in the back." Undoubtedly, the actions of the *minority* of believers had poisoned the opinion of outsiders as to the character of the *majority*.

Maybe you've been hurt by a particular church, denomination, or people within a church. If so, maybe you've equated that wrongful behavior toward you with God's attitude toward you. But that's not who God is. He desires a healthy, love relationship with you. Consider if you are absolutely certain that you have a relationship like this with God through Jesus Christ. If you have any doubt that you have accepted what Jesus did on the cross personally for your sins, and if you're not one hundred percent sure if you have received his free gift of eternal life, this is where to start to experience true peace. If you will pray a simple prayer like this and mean it in your heart, God has promised to save you.

> *Dear Lord, I acknowledge that I have not followed your way. I ask now for you to forgive me of all my sin. I believe that you willingly died on the cross for my sins, rose again, and reign as my Savior; thank you that I am now pure in your sight because of what Jesus did on the cross for me. You love me like no other, and desire to come into my life. I accept your gift of salvation. Guide me, Lord, and grant me peace. Thank you. In Jesus' name. Amen.*

If you just prayed this prayer of salvation for the first time, all of heaven is rejoicing! God has saved you from your sin—past, present, and future. He loves you and is with you! He has come into your life and will never leave you (Hebrews

13:5). This is the most crucial decision you can make because not only will your new relationship with Christ influence your life on earth, but it will also assure you of eternal life (1 John 5:12). Christianity is not about religion; it's a growing relationship with the living God who longs to fellowship with us.

Life drainers

"If anyone comes to me and does not hate his father and mother, his wife and children, his brothers and sisters—yes, even his own life—he cannot be my disciple."

—Luke 14:26

Foreword to Week 5

How's that for a confusing start? Luke 14:26 is not one of the verses you find on Jesus mugs or atop breathtakingly beautiful calendar scenery. It's difficult for us to even *think* in terms of Jesus saying we should hate anything but sin and Satan, but say them he did. Nor can we get around his use of the word by finding alternate translations: the Greek word (*miseo*) means exactly, precisely, what it says…hate.

Only in the context of everything *else* Jesus said about how we are to treat others do we get a more complete picture. For example, if we are to love our enemies, it stands to reason that we should love our spouses as well. "Greater love has no one than this, that he lay down his life for his friends" (John 15:13) sounds like the very antithesis of our memory verse.

It's a matter of degree. In contrast to the all-consuming love for the Lord he commands—"Love the Lord your God with *all* your heart and with *all* your soul and with *all* your strength" (Deuteronomy 6:5, emphasis added)—love for anyone or anything else pales to nothingness. Jesus uses extremes to make a point.

What, you ask, does this have to do with our topic? Life drainers are the people within a congregation who are easiest to ignore, avoid, be irritated by, and even…dare I say it?…*hate*. Their weakness is their strength but not at all in the way Paul intended ("For when I am weak, then I am strong"

2 Corinthians 12:10). The life drainer's insatiable need for attention, counsel, understanding, propping up emotionally, etc. is a powerful force. We must acknowledge the danger of life drainers among us…and the danger of becoming one ourselves.

A friend once commented that there are two kinds of people in the world: givers and takers. Takers are a lot like the goats on our ranch. Boers are an easy-going and beautiful breed, but not what you would call affectionate—they tolerate our presence because we feed and water them and let them eat our pasture grass. With a few exceptions, when we want to pet one—or give one an injection! —it runs the other way.

Goats can get away with it—we are, after all, using them to build a business, not a relationship—but Christians should be known as givers. Life drainers, consumed with themselves (self-love), seem to do nothing *but* take.

Our goal within the church should be involved with being better lifesavers. Narcissism is a spreading, documentable problem in American culture that has no place in the body of Christ. When the emphasis is on "What can you do for me?" it is inevitable that the feelings and needs of some will be overlooked. Life drainers are *baaad* sheep who sap the strength from a church in such a way that others are let down, left to fend for themselves.

Opening Prayer

Father, we are limited in our ability to love even you. How can we possibly love those you've placed around us? Some are especially difficult—help us see them with your eyes. Help us to pour out your love to them without having our energy sapped. Keep us from looking to others to meet all our needs as well, looking instead to you. In Jesus' name we ask these things, Amen.

Positively Negative

Agatha is a very positive person—she'll tell you this without being asked but especially if anyone has the audacity to hint otherwise. She honestly thinks so, too, despite the fact that the slightest sniffle heard in the choir room is a sign of the eminent outbreak of cantata-spoiling pneumonia. Because of her unending sour comments, few people are drawn to her.

"No one likes me," she'll say sadly—until someone feels obliged to prove her wrong and pay her more attention—exactly what she wanted all along.

Compliment someone else and you're guilty of shallow flattery. Mention a health concern, and she's had the same thing…twice and much, much worse. In an attempt to be friendly, you show her the new rug—only to be told that you're likely to catch a heel in the fringe and break your neck, or that she saw the identical item at another store for less money.

Agatha is a life drainer. She's a Christian, absolutely, but a high maintenance, joy-robbing, energy-sapping Christian, the kind that makes outsiders wonder why anyone would want to *become* a believer if she's the best example around.

If she kept to herself, Agatha wouldn't cause so much woe, but she is also one of the most active members, in the choir, on the hospital visitation committee, taking meals to shut-ins. The more people she can be around, you see, the greater supply of life to suck dry. And if confronted about the depressing nature of her words or behavior, she can always fall back on her favorite Scripture: "He was despised and rejected by men, a man of sorrows, and familiar with suffering. Like one from whom men hide their faces he was despised, and we esteemed him not" (Isaiah 53:3).

1 Although hopefully not as skilled in life draining as Agatha, almost every church or organization includes one or two people with similar characteristics. What has been your experience with them?

_____

_____

_____

_____

2 Agatha regards any negative attitude toward her own negativity as taking part in the "fellowship of sharing in (Christ's) suffering" Paul mentioned in Philippians 3:10. What did Paul really mean?

_____

_____

_____

_____

_____

Depressed, oppressed, suppressed...

Recently I walked over to a dear friend at church during the "meet and greet" time. "I'm getting depressed," she said with a frown. Buzzed from Sunday School, coffee, and a few rousing praise songs, I shot her a big grin—"Well, *stop* that!"—gave her a big hug, and went on my way. During worship I became so convicted about my flippancy, I had to ask her forgiveness.

Depression isn't equipped with an on and off button. There are many reasons why it hits—Oswald Chambers wrote that depression comes when we have either satisfied a lust or when we have not.[12] Perhaps this is true in some cases, but surely not in all. Depression can be the result of a significant loss, chemical imbalance, physical illness, *or* hosting a personal pity party that drags on far too long.

* * * * *

Simon spent days in bed, forbidding his wife to even open the curtains. "Why don't you just snap out of it!" she said in frustration. He eventually sought professional help, receiving medication to jumpstart his steps in the right direction and insight into some of the choices that led to the downward spiral. "I'm sorry I couldn't pull myself up by my bootstraps, honey," he told his wife.

* * * * *

Cathy wasn't sure what to do about the cloud hanging over her life and mentioned her dilemma while driving a friend to a meeting one night. Her friend gently pointed out the radio station Cathy had turned to and the Buddha figurine on the dashboard.

It seemed unlikely that such trivialities mattered, but Cathy figured it was worth a try. Praying as she cleaned out the car and her home the next day, she filled garbage bag after garbage bag of things she decided might have a negative spiritual influence on her. The cloud lifted almost immediately.

Demonic oppression is a life drainer from within and one that can also affect our relationships within the church. We shouldn't hunt for demons under every rock, but neither should we ignore the fact that Satan exists and is out to "steal and kill and destroy" (John 10:10).

3 Christians are sometimes made to feel faith-deficient if they take anti-depressants. A family counselor I know says with all the stress in the world today, he's surprised *everyone* isn't on them! What is your opinion on the matter, and why?

_____

_____

_____

_____

_____

4 Discuss Proverbs 25:20 and its relation to dealing with depression.

_____

_____

_____

_____

_____

5 Consider Oswald Chambers' words again. How *could* lust create depression?

_____

_____

_____

_____

_____

6 If Cathy had chosen to laugh off her friend's concerns, what do you think would have happened? Would her feelings of oppression have grown stronger—leading her to eventually reach the same ultimate conclusion—or weaker, becoming so acclimated that she no longer sensed anything wrong? Which would be, spiritually, the greatest danger?

_____

_____

_____

_____

_____

Pick me! Pick me!

Harold left the church fuming, not even bothering to say goodbye to the secretary as he passed her desk. Later, the secretary took some letters in for the pastor to sign. "Recovered yet?"

He sighed. Harold was a regular visitor, never scheduling an appointment, just bursting in with a crying need for counsel or excitement over yet another inspiration. "He had a good idea for an outreach ministry to bikers in the community, but we don't have the resources right now. Plus, the last time he was asked to teach a Sunday School class, he said he didn't have time!"

The secretary shook her head. "My mother always said that if a church won't let you do what *you* think is your ministry, find one that will."

7   Biblical churches follow Ephesians 4 and try to find places for their people to get plugged into ministry. Read verses 11-16, making special note of *so that*'s and *then*'s. What does Paul indicate is the end result?

_____

_____

_____

_____

8   Harold was a life drainer with a cause—leadership was suppressing his God-given talents! How did his attitude reflect a lack of respect for others and their needs?

_____

_____

_____

_____

_____

9 It didn't occur to Harold that perhaps the Lord wanted him to pursue a ministry to bikers on a personal level—since he didn't even own a bike! What kinds of things might he have done with his idea that would lend credibility the next time he approached the pastor for support?

_____

_____

_____

_____

_____

Never pray for patience...

Clara was at the end of her rope. Her sister lived with her due to a debilitating injury; the children constantly needed to be taken hither and yon. The crowning blow came when her husband called with news that he'd been laid off from his job.

Clara's story reminds me of a favorite children's tale: A man goes to his rabbi for advice. He and his wife, two children, a mother-in-law, and a cat lived cramped inside a tiny little house. The rabbi thinks, stroking his beard, and tells him to bring the donkey into the house too.

The man obeys (wondering if the rabbi is growing senile) and returns after a week for further counsel. This time, the rabbi tells him to bring in the chickens as well. The poor man continues for weeks like this, complying with more and more of the same instructions from the rabbi, until he thinks he is going to be driven insane by the noise and chaos, to say nothing of the smell! Practically in tears, he again petitions the rabbi.

The rabbi smiles. "Put out all the animals except for your cat and live in peace."

The man's circumstances at the end of the story are exactly the same as they were at the beginning—what changed was his frame of mind. The saying "It could always be worse" is true. No matter what we are enduring, one *more* thing could go wrong and it would be worse. Our ability to adapt to our circumstances can make them better without anything else actually changing at all.

Clara has choices to make. She can remind herself that God promises not to burden us more heavily than we can bear, that he promises to be with us always, that there would be no need to reward "overcomers" (Revelation 2:7,11,17,26; Revelation 3:5,12,21) if there were nothing *to* overcome in life.

Or she can play the Drama Queen, viewing those around her as life drainers and becoming, in the process, a life drainer herself, constantly complaining to others about her lot in life. When additional bad things come her way (one can almost guarantee they will), her self-pity will be justified anew.

10 The fruit of the Holy Spirit is not just the expected "love, joy, and peace" but also "patience"…also known as "long-suffering" (Galatians 5:22-23). Read Romans 5:3-5. How does "suffering long" lead to hope?

_____

_____

_____

_____

_____

11 Look at Ecclesiastes 7:14-15. How might this give comfort to a life drainer?

_____

_____

_____

_____

_____

12 Consider Anna, the elderly woman who lived in the temple when Jesus was presented to the priest after his birth

(Luke 2:36-38). How might she have become a life drainer, instead of an evangelist?

_____

_____

_____

_____

_____

13 Read Philippians 4:12-13 and discuss as it relates to life drainers and draining circumstances.

_____

_____

_____

_____

_____

Not the Chronic-les of the Bible...

Jesse locked up the building with a sigh, wishing he were seeing more fruit in the lives of the attendees of the church's "12-Step" group. Take Carla, for example. How many times was she going to return to the devastating relationship with her old boyfriend? How many times did he and others have to reassure her of her worth for her to believe it?

Drs. Cloud and Townsend say it like this: "How long is too long? Only you and God know. But it is usually longer than we think."[13] In a way, dealing with people who have chronic issues—possibly the most life-draining people we will ever meet—is the same as walking out forgiveness as Jesus instructed in Matthew 18.

When Peter suggested to Jesus that he should forgive a brother seven times for the same sin, he thought he was being ridiculously generous. Jesus thought otherwise: "Not seven times, but seventy-seven times" (verse 22). The words used could also mean "seventy times seven" and implies a number so high, it can hardly be counted. For the same sin. Every day.

14 Long-term illness, substance abuse, and self-esteem and relationship dynamics are a few of the chronic issues that may face people in church. How have their attitudes and the attitudes of those around them helped or hindered their progress?

_____

_____

_____

_____

15 Children of God are all VIPs (Victory In Progress). How can Philippians 1:6 encourage people with chronic issues as well as those trying to stay afloat emotionally as they deal with them?

_____

_____

_____

_____

_____

More blessed to receive...

When Teresa's husband was hospitalized, many people offered to help if there was anything she needed. "Only one man rang the doorbell and said he was there to cut the grass."

In a sense, the majority of people who were aware of Teresa's predicament acted as life drainers. "They said to call *them*...who had time to pick up a phone, much less write up a list? The brother who came took charge, did what *he* saw was needed. He took all the pressure off of me to initiate action. What a blessing."

* * * * *

Miriam wasn't a life drainer; she was simply drained *by* life as a military wife with four children under the age of five. Then her husband was deployed overseas for a year.

"Christians are great about giving," she says of those long months, "but I had to learn to *receive*. Without being asked, women from the church came every night to help with mealtime and baths. I literally could not have done it without them."

16 James wrote that acceptable religion "[looks] after orphans and widows in their distress" (James 1:27), not mentioning, interestingly enough, any qualifications on their part. Since life drainers are in many ways like emotional children, how might we apply that verse to them?

_____

_____

_____

_____

17 Neither Teresa nor Miriam wanted to impose on anyone, demand help, or whine (as life drainers often do). If they *had*, would they have needed help any less? Would the responsibility of the Christians around them be any different?

_____

_____

_____

_____

_____

Reflection & Encouragement

We should love God the most, but he asks us to love others...often distinctly un-lovely others...as we love ourselves. Loving ourselves includes the idea of being good stewards of our time, talents, and resources. We don't have the luxury of allowing life draining *baaad* sheep to sap energy that God wants directed elsewhere. We can love life drainers, even lay down our lives for them, without letting them control us.

God alone should control our speech and actions—not anyone else, no matter how pitiful they act or how affronted they are by our refusal to be manipulated. And when we find ourselves on the brink of despair, we must look to the Lord to "[lift us] out of the slimy pit, out of the mud and mire...set [our] feet on a rock and [give us] a firm place to stand" (Psalm 40:2).

Nine times out of ten, God will use a Christian brother or sister to act as his hands and feet and mouth, but the emphasis must stay on the Lord. As the old chorus says, "The men of this world will let you down, but Jesus never fails."

Closing Prayer

Lord Jesus, you are the Life and call us to join you in abundant life. There are people around us, however, who would drain that life from us. Keep us strong. Enable us to love them without relinquishing what you died to give us. Help us to lead them to the light, to the only source of true satisfaction and joy. In your name we pray, Amen.

Week 5 Memory Verse

"If anyone comes to me and does not hate his father and mother, his wife and children, his brothers and sisters—yes, even his own life—he cannot be my disciple."
—Luke 14:26

Homework

❶ Are there life drainers in your church, family, or place of business? Make it a point to really listen the next time they speak. Can you discern the real need being expressed? If it is possible to meet that need, do it...with a smile.

_____

_____

_____

_____

_____

❷ Practice saying "No." Church programs are often life-draining entities in and of themselves. Are you spending more time on them than with your family? Are you getting adequate rest and time alone? Stand at a mirror and picture yourself being asked...and just say no! "I already have plans for Tuesday evenings." "No, I don't think that will work out." "I'm sorry, but I'm committed to something else right now."

❸ Take a personal inventory: have you acted as a life drainer with anyone in your life? Be a blessing instead, with a card, gift, or phone call (no expectations or requests included).

❹ Do Week Six to prepare for next week.

Criminals & other commandment-breakers

"For you were once darkness, but now you are light in the Lord. Live as children of light (for the fruit of the light consists in all goodness, righteousness and truth) and find out what pleases the Lord."

—*Ephesians 5:8-10*

Foreword to Week 6

Sin, as they say, is sin. Before we come to a saving knowledge of Jesus Christ, it is our nature to sin, to break commandments, to bend both divine and civil laws for our own purposes. After we become Christians, however, we are to "live as children of light." Unfortunately, problems with sin continue after salvation and baptism. Old, *baaad* habits die hard. Addictions are rarely forsaken overnight. The heart of man (and woman) will go to extreme lengths to justify bad behavior.

Because of poor choices prior to (or after) salvation, there are also Christian criminals…or more accurately, criminals in the eyes of the law who profess Christ. A parolee may share your pew. You may have a deacon with a DUI. Someone in children's ministry may have to serve time for defaulting on child *support*. When we discover such information, we may feel let down for a number of reasons: we were clueless and so, feel stupid; it hurts our pride in "our" congregation; it forces us to examine our hearts for the proper responses; etc.

The upside is that if we've got criminals—former or current—in our congregation, we must be doing something right…we're attracting the very kinds of people Jesus did while on earth!

Our response to the *baaad* sheep that have broken the laws of God and/or man is important. And if we are guilty ourselves, our response to correction is even more significant.

Opening Prayer

Father, open our eyes to your light. Expose the sin in our lives and give us eyes to see the world around us as you see it. Where your law is broken, help us to restore it. Help us to restore also the one who has fallen into sin, or to be restored ourselves. In Jesus' name, Amen.

First, America's Most Wanted...

We don't normally think of church as a haven for criminals, but we're all sinners in need of forgiveness and grace. Those with rap sheets simply have a more public, more visible need. When Rocky was arrested for drug trafficking, evidence left little doubt concerning his guilt. Members wanted to be supportive, but some felt duped. Had he sold drugs to any of the youth? Given drug money to the church? Lied about his conversion?

* * * * *

In a totally different setting, Seth arrived at a mission base and was welcomed as a fellow believer by the entire staff. He said all the right things, humbly asking for assistance. Strapped for funds themselves, the group nevertheless offered food and shelter and enough money for essentials.

The next day, Seth disappeared—and not with just the clothes on his back or the small amount of cash he'd been given. Despite their genuine desire to help a brother, the base staff had been royally ripped off.

In the first example, the crime had nothing to do with church. Rocky had not, in fact, let greed directly affect his relationship with church members or their children. He was repentant, making no excuses for past deeds that finally caught up with him. When he stood before the judge, a group of supporters stood with him, many of whom were believers. There would be jobs waiting when he got out, help for his wife and children during his incarceration, letters of encouragement. Today, Rocky remains spiritually strong and remembers the love of Christians, during one of the hardest times of his life, with humility and gratitude.

In the second example, the church fell victim to a criminal—a wolf in sheep's clothing. It is possible that Seth had at one time made a commitment to the Lord but he had learned to use his knowledge of "Christian-ese" for personal gain. Those who helped him felt used and stupid. A few questioned their spiritual I.Q.—why hadn't discernment kicked in?

1 We don't take it well when someone steals from us, lies to us, or commits a crime that directly affects us. Trust is a fragile commodity—once damaged, it may never recover. How did Rocky's attitude and behavior pave the way for reconciliation?

_____

_____

_____

_____

_____

2 The Bible instructs us to give to those who ask (Matthew 5:42) without explaining specific qualifications. But it also cautions us against "throw[ing] your pearls to pigs" (Matthew 7:6). Were Seth's victims obedient to the Word? What might they have done differently?

_____

_____

_____

_____

_____

3 How much does context affect our interpretation of crime? Is speeding to a hospital less of a crime than speeding to a movie? During World War II, the laws of Nazi Germany were contrary to the laws of God—were "criminals" who aided Jews more honorable than the "law-abiding" citizens who allowed Hitler to implement his Final Solution? What of today's criminals who target abortion centers? If they believe America is in a war for the unborn, should that affect their punishment when arrested for criminal behavior such as bombing a clinic?

_____

_____

_____

_____

_____

4 Look at Mark 2:17 and discuss its relevance to this session.

_____

_____

_____

_____

_____

American Idol, revisited...

For the first time, I got hooked on the 2006 season's talent search program "American Idol." From the first audition session that aired, the weekly screenings, performances, voting, and booing of Simon (whom I rather liked), it was "must-see TV."

But what a name: American IDOL. Ick. No doubt there were folks more spiritual than I who boycotted the show for just that reason. "Idol" can mean either an image of a god, the god itself, or any object of worship—judging from the fan base across the country and my own household's ardent attention, perhaps the name is fitting.

Something within us compels us to worship, needs to elevate someone or something to a place of prominence. King Solomon wrote that God "has…set eternity in the hearts of men" (Ecclesiastes 3:11). Paul had no sympathy for those who do not believe in God: "…what may be known about God is plain to them, because God has *made* it plain to them. For since the creation of the world God's invisible qualities—his eternal power and divine nature—have been clearly seen, being understood from what has been made, so that men are without excuse" (Romans 1:19-20, emphasis added).

When we don't accept God for who he is and worship *him*, Satan has a whole slew of substitutes lined up to take his place. A young woman once asked a visiting speaker if she would have to give up dancing to become a Christian. To the surprise of those who knew him, he answered in the affirmative. When questioned, he explained it wasn't the dancing. She could have mentioned any number of things—dancing just happened to be the thing she worshipped.

Is there idolatry in the church today? Undeniably. Some congregations worship their pastors, youth worship Christian singers, couch quarterbacks spend far more time following their favorite teams than following the Lord. There is an abundance of good church folks who won't give up their favorite possession, prejudice, or person even if the finger of God wrote it on their living room walls. Whatever or whomever has the top spot on our priority list is our god, and woe unto us if we can't capitalize that G.

Jesus is either Lord *of* all (in our lives) or he is not Lord *at* all. When young Christians, struggling Christians, or non-Christians hear us announcing our salvation, we'd better not contradict ourselves by worshipping someone or something else.

5 Would God lead one of his children to become an Idol? At least one of the 2006 American Idol finalists was a Christian who used her time in the spotlight both to witness and to *be* a witness. Many professional athletes use their celebrity status to spread the gospel. Discuss the opportunities and pitfalls of fame.

_____

_____

_____

_____

6 Isaiah gave a graphic description of the absurdity of worshipping idols—read chapter 44, verses 12-20 and relate it to common "idols" today, both religious and worldly.

_____

_____

_____

What's in a name?

It's been a long time since my mother had little ones underfoot, but she still volunteers to baby-sit. Once she left the house after a particularly trying marathon stay with her great-granddaughter Jasmine, an active toddler at the time. "We should pray for G.G. She really needs God," Jasmine solemnly announced at dinner. When questioned further, she said, "All day long, G.G. kept saying, 'God help me, God help me.'" "G.G." was no doubt muttering genuine supplication, but we hear God's name thrown about so often that most of us have become jaded.

> **Church Sign Display**
>
> *If you're going to cuss,*
> *use your own name.*

As a teenager, I stood with a friend of mine and his mother at a small airport. The sudden noise of an approaching plane startled him; without thinking he sputtered, "Jesus, that's loud!" His mother quietly said, "That name is awfully special to me. I'd appreciate it if you wouldn't use it that way." Her reverence made a lasting impression on me.

What was God really after with this commandment—the proper use of a word or the proper representation of his character? When we represent ourselves as Christians and then behave contrary to God's Word, we are taking his name in vain with much potential for negative affect.

The original meaning of "profane" is to treat a holy object as common. Thus, when Paul wrote that there shouldn't be "obscenity, foolish talk or coarse joking which are out of place" (Ephesians 5:4) among Christians, he referred to a sign of spiritual error rather than just a nasty habit. If we regard God as holy, and by extension, his creation and the institutions he set forth, we should recognize that what our grandmothers might have called "potty mouth" was indeed profanity—reducing something holy to something common.

7 Do you know anyone with a problem in this area?

_____

_____

_____

_____

_____

8 Jesus said that making oaths is evil (Matthew 5:33-37). James pointed out the duplicity of using our mouths for both blessing and cursing (James 3:9-12). Discuss practical ways a person could overcome these habits.

_____

_____

_____

_____

_____

9 A carpenter made it a point to tell a client what a good Christian the carpenter himself was, but then he did a shabby job and charged an unreasonably high price. The client decided he'd never hire a "Christian" again. In your experience, do Christian businesses that advertise their faith with fish symbols, Scriptures on business cards, etc. further the cause of Christ? Share positive and negative results.

_____

_____

_____

_____

_____

Just another day...

Whenever people say Christians have concocted a god in their own image, I have to chuckle. If I were making up a god, he certainly wouldn't have made it a law to rest _one_ day out of seven. I'd much rather have two or three. The Chosen People, however, were given the Sabbath.

Somewhere along the line, Christians began worshipping on the first day of the week to honor the resurrection, but Paul inferred that one day was just as good as the next (Romans 14:5-8). Hebrews talks of the Sabbath rest in terms of allowing us to enter into God's rest now that the work of the cross is complete (see Hebrews 4).

Our church sponsors a children's program during the school year that includes fun and games but emphasizes Scripture memorization. One parent told a leader that his own childhood experience with the program hadn't been positive. It seems his parents would take a nice long nap every Sunday afternoon—while the kids spent hours toiling over their weekly verses! No rest for the kids.

In older days, sometimes Sundays were endured, rather than enjoyed. Long serious services were followed by sitting upright in uncomfortable chairs and reading the Bible—very little "rejoicing" going on, which misses the point. God *made* us. He is "familiar with all (our) ways" (Psalm 139:3). The Sabbath was given as a blessing, not a punishment.

10 God knows our nature; if we didn't have a divinely ordained prescription for a day of rest, many workaholics would *never* spend time with their families. If you didn't go to church on Sunday, what would you be doing with your time?

_____

_____

_____

_____

_____

11 Entering God's "Sabbath rest" (Hebrews 4) means more than setting a day aside. Discuss in your group what God intended a "Sabbath rest" to mean. How have various misinterpretations of the commandment hurt the cause of Christ? Have any helped?

_____

_____

_____

_____

_____

12 Discuss ways in which our culture is geared toward obedience of this command—the typical work week, "blue
laws" of the past (and in some areas, the present), etc.

_____

_____

_____

_____

_____

Hello mudda, hello fadda...

James Jr. had taken a new job out of state when his wid-
owed father was hospitalized. Several members of his former
church organized a group to insure that James Sr. had a
steady stream of visitors and, once back at home, regular
meals and follow-up care. When Junior finally showed up, he
had plenty of negative things to say but expressed very little
gratitude. Melinda couldn't believe her ears. "We were taking
care of his father when he wouldn't or couldn't, and he never
even said 'thank you.'"

* * * * *

Penny's mother wasn't at Sunday School one particular
morning, and Penny mentioned her mother's depression during prayer request time—going into quite a lot of detail. Commented one listener later, "It reminded me of those Old Testament verses about children 'uncovering their father's naked-
ness.' I was embarrassed on her mother's behalf."

* * * * *

Jacqueline turned the overhead light off as she visited
with her friend in the living room. "Trying to keep the utility
bill down." It was obvious her lifestyle was sparse.

"Doesn't your son still live in town?" the friend asked.
"He's doing quite well for himself, I hear."

Jacqueline's eyes flashed. "Yes, I hear the same thing. He
gives quite a lot of money to his church, goes to meetings

practically every night there." She sighed sadly, "But he has-n't brought my grandchildren to see me in over a month."

Even in today's complicated world of frequent divorces and remarriages, most of us relate primarily to one set of parents. We have fathers; we have mothers. God said it is important to honor them. In fact, the fourth commandment is the one commandment with a promise: "Honor your father and your mother, as the Lord your God has commanded you, so that you may live long and that it may go well with you in the land the Lord your God is giving you" (Deuteronomy 6:16).

With all the emphasis in our culture on long life, you rarely hear about the importance of honoring one's parents, but God made that very thing a prerequisite for longevity and success. When we dishonor our parents, it's like telling God we'd just as soon die young as an utter failure.

Parents, like all the *baaad* sheep of our discussions, let us down. They are not perfect, were not perfect when we were children, may have disappointed, used, abused, or abandoned us. Whether their characters warrant our respect or not, their positions do…if we are serious about obeying God's Word.

Do we have to be manipulated to honor? No. Should we categorically, as adults, *obey* our parents? Not at all. The command is to honor, as simple as a phone call once in awhile or as major as becoming adult caretakers when a parent becomes feeble.

Apparently young Timothy had some *baaad* sheep in his fold, for Paul instructed him to light a fire under them, so to speak. "If a widow has children or grandchildren, these should learn first of all to put their religion into practice by caring for their own family and so repaying their parents and grandparents, for this is pleasing to God" (1 Timothy 5:4).

13 A lifestyle of dishonoring parents definitely lets *the parents* down. How have cultural shifts away from close-knit, patriarch-headed, family units also had a far-reaching negative affect on society?

14 How did the examples of James, Penny, and Jacqueline's son reflect the spiritual (im)maturity of each?

15 As a teenager, Amy was abused by her father. Now married with children of her own, a counselor encouraged her to confront him; she fears she isn't ready and has concerns for her daughters' safety. Experts on sexual abuse recommend confrontation only when it can be done from a position of strength. Even in such a terrible situation, what are some concrete ways Amy could honor her father without giving him continued power over her emotions?

Super-size sin...

Murder and adultery are considered by many of us to be the most heinous crimes on the Big Ten list, perhaps because both involve death. Murder takes away a person's breath; adultery often snuffs out a marriage.

It's interesting that in the Sermon on the Mount, Jesus used these two commandments to introduce his radical concept of fulfilling the Law. "You have heard that it was said...but I tell you..." (Matthew 5:21-22,27-28).

The Jews already knew not to commit murder, but Jesus instructed them not to assassinate each others' *spirits* by calling them derogatory names. They already knew adultery was a no-no, but Jesus told them that merely *lusting* after women was equally wrong.

I'm not 100% sure, but I'd hazard a guess that I don't know a single murderer. I know *lots* of people (self included) who have been known to ridicule and name-call—we may not be breaking a civil law when we do so, may not be on the FBI's Most Wanted List for calling someone a "jerk" who pulls out ahead of us in traffic, but consider Jesus' strong words: "Anyone who says, 'You fool!' will be in danger of the fire of hell" (Matthew 5:22).

Adultery can send us to H-E-double hockey sticks too. "Do you not know that the wicked will not inherit the kingdom of God? Do not be deceived: Neither the sexually immoral nor idolaters nor adulterers nor male prostitutes nor homosexual offenders nor thieves nor the greedy nor drunkards nor slanderers nor swindlers will inherit the kingdom of God. And that is what some of you were. But you were washed, you were sanctified, you were justified in the name of the Lord Jesus Christ and by the Spirit of our God" (1 Corinthians 6:9-11).

Paul started meddling and just couldn't stop! At least he ended on a positive note—that's what some of you *were*, he said. Unfortunately, in the church today we have problems *now* with the very things on his list. Statistically, there is just as much immorality among teens inside the church as outside. As much abortion. As many adulterous affairs. As much divorce.

Craig and Lisa sang on the worship team at their church; proximity as well as similar interests led them to develop a deep friendship. "She made me wonder if God actually *did* have a wife for me," Craig said. "And I really listened to her—there were lots of problems at home." Eventually, almost imperceptibly, their relationship crossed an invisible line.

Lisa remembered the day she became convicted of adultery. "We hadn't even kissed," she exclaimed, "but my heart transferred from my husband to Craig. I looked for advice and affirmation from him."

When Lisa shared this realization with Craig, he was defensive. He hadn't done anything wrong...or had he? As he prayed, the Holy Spirit convicted him as well. He had thought he was helping out a friend he'd grown to love. "I had no *right* to love her that way."

* * * * *

Studies show that up to 40% of Christians will have an extramarital affair by the time they have been married twenty years. Catherine's affair was devastating. Although she was fully convinced that her marriage to Bill was of God, she found herself toying with the notion that perhaps God had changed his mind. Bill was unloving. He didn't notice her or seem to care that other men found her attractive.

"If you looked up 'taken for granted' in a dictionary, my photo would've been there. I was like a tree withering in the sun. Someone came along and watered me—and if it hadn't been Sam, I'm sure it would've been someone else."

With counseling, Bill and Catherine's marriage survived, but it has taken years to rebuild trust—and not just Bill's trust of Catherine. "If he goes a few days without showing affection, there's a temptation to think 'Oh, here we go again.' I have to remember that God is working on *both* of us. And I have to ultimately look to the *Lord* to meet my needs."

Church friends responded in strange ways, explained Catherine. "I was treated like a leper, as if Bill wasn't accountable at all." Bill added, "As the spiritual head of my household, I let the family down by not being the husband and father God intended. But in most peoples' eyes, I think, I was simply the victim."

16 Read 1 John 3:15-20—considering John's standard, do you know any murderers? By these standards, have you been a murderer?

_____

_____

_____

_____

_____

17 In God's eyes, were Craig and Lisa as guilty of adultery—both admitted to lustful feelings—as Catherine, who physically committed the sin? No one was aware that anything inappropriate was taking place with Craig and Lisa, however, while Catherine was the brunt of "mountains" of gossip. How do the perceptions of others affect your level of conviction?

_____

_____

_____

_____

_____

18 Bill took responsibility for his own actions and attitudes. What impact do you think this had on their marriage?

_____

_____

_____

_____

_____

God's standard for honesty...

"I hate this problem I'm having with lying," Phil told the pastor.

"But you don't hate *lying*," the pastor replied.

Point well taken. If we truly hate something, we usually stop. If we tolerate sin in our lives, however, we will search far and wide, high and low, for ways to justify it, skating around the possibility of harsh consequences. As speaker Doug Easterday says, Christians don't usually fall into sin, we *jump* into it...like kids jumping into a pile of autumn leaves. Wheeee...

Honesty isn't just the best policy; it's the *only* policy for Christians. 100% honesty, 100% of the time. *No* lying, *no* stealing. No using stamps from the office for personal mail just this once. No "white lie" about one's whereabouts last Thursday evening.

Is honesty a problem in the church? I dare say that it is. Perhaps attendance numbers are inflated on a report, or a sermon is appropriated, word for word, from the Internet without giving honor where it is due. Perhaps someone speaks an untruth to avoid hurting someone's feelings. But when we discover that a brother or sister has lied to us, we feel let down. If he or she lied about that, what else can we not trust?

Satan is called a "liar and the father of lies" (John 8:44). Not the kind of company we should keep.

19 Discuss the similarities and differences between deception and lying and ways in which you (or others you know) have been hurt by this sin in the church setting.

_____

_____

_____

_____

_____

I want, I want...

If you've ever taken a child to Wal-Mart, you've been well-schooled in covetousness. Every sugary morsel, every bright object, anything remotely resembling a toy, and the mantra taught by every television commercial known to man begins, "I want that! Can I have that? Pleeeeeeeeeze?"

* * * * *

Mandy was a single mother of two; across the street lived her friend Paula, a happily married mother of three. Mandy found herself resenting everything Paula said, even the helpful way she offered to do things for her.

* * * * *

At church, Clyde caught a glimpse of his buddy's new girlfriend as they sat down in the sanctuary. "Man," he thought, "I wish my wife looked that good."

* * * * *

Melissa had spent the year as a missionary overseas and was traveling home in the morning. The electricity in the building had been off for hours. Tired from packing, Melissa fumed, "I was really looking forward to a hot shower."

"You can take all the hot showers you want soon enough," a fellow missionary snapped.

* * * * *

At age four, our oldest daughter was diagnosed with Juvenile Rheumatoid Arthritis. For years, if I heard someone give a glowing testimony of divine healing, jealousy would rear its ugly head. If God healed in that situation, why was there no healing for *our* child?

Covetousness is easy to conceal—if a person were to voice his lust for someone's spouse or house or car or kids or money or job, he'd look petty and jealous. God sees our hearts, however. He knows when covetousness lurks behind innocuous words or actions. He knows when "the cravings of sinful man, the lust of his eyes and the boasting of what he has and does" (1 John 2:16) has come into play.

When we observe covetousness in others, it's offensive, a letdown...for the same reasons we try to keep our own under wraps. Things we covet are different than things we need—God promises to meet our needs, but not our wants...and certainly not our lusts.

20 Jesus told his disciples to gouge out an eye rather than lust after a woman, to cut off a hand rather than risk going to hell (Matthew 5:29,30). Assuming he was speaking figuratively (!), he nevertheless called for drastic measures to avoid sin. To what extremes might he call a Christian to go to in order to avoid, say, a neighbor who arouses lust? A friendship with someone who encourages sinful behavior? A job that involves unscrupulous business practices?

_____

_____

_____

_____

_____

21 We can covet even godly things. Sara is a talented singer. On several occasions, others have "confessed" to wishing God could use them that way. "The way it was worded, though, it almost sounded like they'd rather I never sang, so they'd feel better about themselves!" Sara said. Have you ever coveted a spiritual gift or testimony or had someone obviously covet yours?

_____

_____

_____

_____

Reflection & Encouragement

God gave the Jews over four hundred laws but narrowed them down to ten. In Matthew 22, Jesus narrowed it down to two: (1) "Love the Lord your God with all your heart and with all your soul and with all your mind" and (2) "Love your neighbor as yourself." If we keep *these* commandments, we're far less likely to break the others.

It's a big "if," though, isn't it? We break the laws of man (hopefully in only minor ways) and God (with whom there *is* no minor or major, really) on a daily basis, failing to hit the bull's eye, which is complete obedience, with any kind of consistency. When *we* fail, we want grace and mercy. When *others* fail, we demand justice!

Although Jesus announced from the cross that his work on earth was finished (John 19:30), his work within the church is *far* from over. Paul and Timothy urged us to remain confident of the fact that "he who began a good work in you will carry it on to completion until the day of Christ Jesus" (Philippians 1:6). It's a good time to remind ourselves that he promised the same thing to the *baaad* sheep in our lives.

Closing Prayer

Holy Father, we acknowledge our inability to keep your law, even when it boils down to only one command: to love you as we ought. Thank you for your commitment to continue to train and guide us. Our brothers and sisters are in the same boat—none of them complete either. Give us grace to extend mercy as we also deal with them wisely, just as we ask for mercy from you. In Jesus' name, Amen.

Week 6 Memory Verse

"For you were once darkness, but now you are light in the Lord. Live as children of light (for the fruit of the light consists in all goodness, righteousness and truth) and find out what pleases the Lord."

—Ephesians 5:8-10

Homework

❶ Pray about any indiscretion that continues to nag your conscience. It may be as minor as making copies at work without putting money into petty cash. With today's technology, it may involve illegally downloaded DVDs or CDs. Consider whether Jesus would have you deal with it *drastically*, and make necessary restitution.

❷ Take an inventory of commandment-breakers around you. Have there been mitigating circumstances? Do you have a responsibility to confront or correct?

_____

_____

_____

_____

_____

❸ Pray especially for the group as it approaches the next session. Due to the sensitive nature of the session's content, emotions may run higher than previously. Pray for extra wisdom and guidance for your group leader as well.

❹ Do Week Seven to prepare for next week.

Wolves in sheep's (and shepherds') clothing

"Now the overseer must be above reproach...."
—*1 Timothy 3:2a*

Foreword to Week 7

Prior to beginning work on this particular session, I laid aside the project for several weeks due to a trip and obligations elsewhere. It's usually a little frustrating to be in the middle of something and have it interrupted, but in this case, it was the Lord's provision—I needed a little R & R before tackling the monsters in *this* closet.

We've looked at many of the ways in which God's people, his sheep, behave *baaadly* toward one another. The results of gossip, manipulation, lying, adultery, and whatnot may remain hidden or may be turned into public spectacles. They may be trivial, requiring nothing more than the shake of the head and an "Oh, well" to get past. They may run deep, requiring drastic measures to overcome. In comparison to the hurts caused by sheep that are also *shepherds*, however, much of what we have discussed is relatively minor.

Matthew 7:15-23 is, in my opinion, one of the (if not *the*) scariest passages in the Bible: "'Watch out for false prophets. They come to you in sheep's clothing but inwardly they are ferocious wolves....' 'Not everyone who says to me, "Lord, Lord," will enter the kingdom of heaven, but only he who does the will of my Father who is in heaven. Many will say to me on that day, "Lord, Lord, did we not prophesy in your name, and in your name drive out demons and perform many miracles?" Then I will tell them plainly, "I never knew you. Away from me, you evildoers!"'"

A person may do all the right things, say all the right things, and *still not be* one of the Lord's disciples. Despite outward signs of anointing, displays of supernatural power—all presumably in the name of the Lord Jesus Christ—at the end, he will cast them from his presence. If that doesn't put a healthy fear of God in you, I don't know what will.

Just as evildoers existed in the world two thousand years ago, they exist today. Paul urged us to stay away from those bringing "a different gospel": "Such men are false apostles, deceitful workmen, masquerading as apostles of Christ. And no wonder, for Satan himself masquerades as an angel of light. It is not surprising then, if his servants masquerade as servants of righteousness. Their end will be what their actions deserve" (2 Corinthians 11:4, 13-15).

But this study is devoted to the discussion of sheep, not charlatans. *Baaad* though they are, they are also still believers, men and women in leadership who sincerely love the Lord and are, like the rest of us, incomplete works, victories in progress, sojourners on the way to glory. They have specific areas of weakness and deception in their own lives, and are tempted and oppressed by the enemy of our souls.

Like King David, the "man after (God's) own heart" (1 Samuel 13:14), who later committed adultery and murder, they truly serve God. As representatives of God and shepherds of his flock, however, the hurts they cause carry more potential to devastate. No wonder Paul instructed Timothy to only delegate God's authority to those "without reproach."

Because the enemy uses sinful leaders to let down so many people in one fell swoop and perpetrate so much havoc in the body of Christ, it is essential that we shine the light on deeds the church has historically kept behind closed doors. Expose sin, and God is glorified. Expose darkness within, and we will all have a safer pasture in which to feed. "For it is time for judgment to begin with the family of God" (1 Peter 4:17a).

Opening Prayer

Father, there is none righteous but you. We judge our own hearts in your presence, asking you to reveal the things that are displeasing to you. And we ask, for the sake of your glory and for the sake of the purity of the Bride of Christ, that you give us eyes to see where evil dwells, whether it is in our own hearts, or standing behind a pulpit. Heal those who have been hurt by leaders claiming to act in your name. Bring leaders in sin to repentance. Give the church the courage to take a stand for righteousness. In Jesus' holy name we pray, Amen.

Head of gold...

In the Old Testament, we find the story of a heathen monarch who wanted his dream interpreted. After much prayer, Daniel, one of a group of young Jewish captives, was able not only to reveal the meaning of King Nebuchadnezzar's dream, but also describe it in detail.

The dream, Daniel began, had centered on a large statue with a head of gold, chest and arms of silver, belly and thighs of bronze, legs of iron, and feet of iron and clay. The statue was destroyed. His interpretation began with a reminder that God was the one who had given the king his authority, dramatically leading up to the words, "You are that head of gold."

At that point, Nebuchadnezzar probably stopped listening. Who cared what happened to the kingdom after his, or the kingdoms after that? *He was the head of gold.* It had a nice ring to it. (See Daniel 2 for the complete story.)

People in positions of authority face a similar temptation to embrace the accompanying *privileges* without focusing on their *responsibilities.* A CEO who is only concerned about his or her Swiss bank accounts will bend and break laws to the point of destroying the corporation. A president without moral convictions will make poor decisions in his private life that eventually affect public service. A sheriff who takes on the job for paycheck and prestige rather than as a champion for community safety will create turmoil in his department with a trickle-down effect leading to increased crime.

And a pastor...or youth leader...or parish priest...who enjoys the esteem of people more than the approval of God may well turn into a predator of the very sheep God entrusted into his or her care. Peter instructed the elders of the church to serve without greed or pride and to be *examples* to the flock (1 Peter 5:2-3). I'm fairly certain he meant *good* examples, not bad examples.

1   A commercial airline pilot once remarked that all good pilots are cocky because flying well requires self-confidence. How could a spiritual leader's confidence in God-given abilities be twisted by pride?

_____

_____

_____

2 Churches sometimes make the mistake of putting new Christians in positions of leadership because they are so enthusiastic. What are some of the problems that can result? Discuss the qualifications found in 1 Timothy 3.

_____

_____

_____

_____

_____

Minor flaws are major...

It's got to be tough, living under the microscopic examination of not only the public, but also the people in one's congregation too. Having lived on the mission field long enough to understand the feeling of being under constant surveillance, I don't envy those who have chosen the role of pastor or pastor's spouse. PKs (Preachers' Kids) don't have much say in the matter; I feel for them most of all.

As I've mentioned, those with positions of authority are really no different than your common, garden-variety believer, but they are *scrutinized* more closely. Scripture says in James 3:1 that those leaders who are teachers will be judged more strictly. Just as Christians are judged severely by the world because we claim a higher standard, Christian leaders are judged even moreso—after all, they *bring* the standard.

Dawson's wife is a gung-ho church member. Dawson used to attend semi-regularly, but ever since the pastor burned up the engine in the truck he borrowed, whatever enthusiasm there was has been replaced by disdain. "I was brought up to return things in a *better* condition than when I borrowed them," he said. "First, he burns up the engine, then he calls *me* to tow him back from across the state. And I'm supposed to be all sweetness and light about it 'cause he's the preacher."

* * * * *

When Kate asked Jared to go with her to the minister for marriage counseling, he had a notion it would turn out badly.

He really wanted things to work out, however, so he agreed. "She and the minister had already drawn up a long list of what I was doing wrong. I have no problem working on my end of things, but to hear him tell it, she came straight out of Proverbs 31. Wouldn't let me so much as ask a question."

* * * * *

Pastor Pete has the annoying habit of referring to himself from the pulpit in the third person. "Pastor wants all of you to know…," he'll start. Pam's weren't the only teeth he set on edge, but when he started criticizing his son in public, she felt she needed to "have it out" with him. Not surprised at his pompous response, she didn't regret making the appointment. "I love him in the Lord," Pam said, shaking her head. "All I can do is try to help him see things from our perspective. What he does with it is up to the Lord…and the board. And I sure wish he'd stop with that infernal 'Pastor wants this' and 'Pastor wants that.'"

Minor grievances, certainly. Errors in judgment, a lack of proper training, most definitely. Because we are human, we can expect to have disagreements with leadership from time to time—even actual conflicts. Such occurrences can reach frustrating levels, easily turned into opportunities for politicking, maneuvering, gossip, and the like, and we need to deal with these moments in a godly way. Sometimes, however—with a tiny minority of those in leadership—sinful behavior escalates to a *frightening* level.

3 Dawson has no intention of pursuing a commitment to the Lord if it means sitting under his wife's pastor's teaching. How might his wife help "win him over without a word" (see 1 Peter 3:1) in this situation?

_____

_____

_____

_____

_____

4 Pastors do not all receive the same level of "people skills" training. What characteristics do you consider to be especially important for their job description?

_____

_____

_____

_____

_____

5 Elders and deacons have a special calling to minister to
their ministers; some churches establish prayer chains
specifically for their pastors' wives and families. Discuss
other ways to help those in leadership.

_____

_____

_____

_____

_____

Fleecing the kids...

Darren enjoyed the youth group he was attending, although he wasn't sure about the "commitment to Jesus" stuff.
Unfortunately, any time he raised his hand to ask a question,
the group's leader, a fellow named Ray, who was just out of
college, acted as if Darren was trying to be a problem. It did-
n't help matters that Darren stood a head taller than Ray or
that his natural leadership abilities drew others to him.

Ray acted like he had all the answers, but never the ones
Darren needed. Darren finally stopped by the preacher's office to talk. After he left, the preacher called Ray and suggested he pay closer attention to his youth. "That's what
we're paying you for," he added.

After the next meeting, Ray asked Darren to stick around.
"I don't appreciate you going over my head," he told the boy.
When Darren turned to leave, Ray shouted at him, "Don't
walk away from me," throwing down a chair in anger. Before
long, the two were scuffling.

* * * * *

Lydia was concerned that some of the more clique-ish
members in the youth group would ignore Sandi, a visitor.
"Make it a point to be nice to her," she asked a few of the
girls. Not only did they speak to Sandi, they repeated Lydia's

request word for word. "I'm never going back," Sandi darkly told her mother later. "Everyone goes on about what good Christians those kids are, but they have to be *told* to be nice to me? I don't think so."

Sandi's mother related the conversation to Lydia, asking the leader to seek her out and explain her motivation. "If Sandi's mad, she can come and talk to me," Lydia replied. Sandi's mother reminded her that as a leader, she had the opportunity to be more mature, to make the first move, to reach out to a troubled teenager. She's still waiting for Lydia to do so; Sandi never returned.

* * * * *

When Marilyn was about 20 years old, she found a small church back in her home town that reminded her of the congregation she had enjoyed while at college. Technically too old for the youth group, she was invited to take part as there was no young adult class at the time. Often, she'd drop by the church-run bookstore during her lunch hour and step into the youth pastor's office to chat.

One day while talking in his office, the youth pastor said, "Kiss me, Marilyn." When she tried to laugh it off, he repeated the command. "I mean it...*kiss me*."

Marilyn fumbled around for words and backed out of the office. The experience threw her completely off balance and she looked for another church. "I wish I'd told someone, because I later heard he'd tried the same thing with one of the younger girls."

6   Leadership is a wonderful place for someone who is humble, but not for someone with self-doubt and low self-esteem. Ray approached his job with a chip on his shoulder; Darren seemed to be constantly trying to knock the chip off. If Ray were to remain the youth leader and you were his employer, what steps would you require him to take?

_____

_____

_____

_____

_____

7 The preacher had compassion toward Darren, patiently answering his questions. Did he show compassion toward Ray? What might he have done differently, with more positive results?

_____

_____

_____

_____

_____

8 Sandi's response shows she expected the youth group girls to be better behaved than they were. Why?

_____

_____

_____

_____

9 How far should Lydia go to draw Sandi into the group? How far would *you* go?

_____

_____

_____

_____

10 Youth leaders are sometimes viewed as glorified baby-sitters. In reality, their service is of huge importance in the life of the church. How does a church's mentality toward its youth and children's ministry affect the quality of those who fill those positions?

_____

_____

_____

_____

_____

11 Power can act as an aphrodisiac. Marilyn's youth pastor may have been gifted in other areas of leadership, but clearly, either lust for control, sexual lust, or a combination of both was a problem. Marilyn is now in her forties—how has the social climate changed in favor of protecting the innocent?

_____

_____

_____

_____

_____

12 What kind of personal issues—or lies from the enemy—might stop a person from confronting the perpetrator in such a situation?

_____

_____

_____

_____

_____

Emily's story...

"Pastoral abuse" is an oxymoron—in its most basic meaning, pastoring involves nurturing and caring for others, the sense of which is found in Jesus' words to Peter after the resurrection: "Feed my lambs...take care of my sheep...feed my sheep" (John 21:15-18). Abuse of that role could include such things as bringing unbalanced teaching, failure to follow up with or pray for members, or a zillion other disappointments that can easily occur within a very human and often overworked clergy. What generally comes to mind when we hear the term (or see it splashed across headlines), however, is sex.

One of God's greatest gifts, misused by one of his other great gifts—spiritual leadership.

None of us is immune to the temptation of sexual sin, but leaders are in a position to cause far more damage to a congregation, even to an entire community, than most. Whether it is "fair" or not, our memory/meditation verse gives us (and the rest of the world) a scriptural basis for expecting church leaders to behave according to the highest possible standards.

Emily was introduced in Session Four. Her story follows—not because it describes the worst case of pastoral abuse around, but having known her personally, I understand her heart, the doubts she's overcome, the sense of her own failures and responsibilities, and God's awesome restorative power in her life. As with other illustrations, names and details have been changed to protect both the innocent and guilty.

> *As a child, we started going to Pastor Glen's church and made friends with his family. He visited our home often—many times when Dad wasn't there—and there was just something about him I didn't like. His sermons challenged me to read the Bible and pray more, and for the first time, I really committed myself to God, but something seemed "off."*
>
> *Glen went out of his way to win me over, though. I must have been around 14 when I was upset about a decision—it was nothing, really. I'd ridden with his group to a youth trip and he signed me up to ride home with another. When he saw me pouting, he said, "Well, we could kiss and make up." If I'd made a big deal out of what he said, I'm sure he would have said it was a joke, but it bothered me. I decided to tell him he shouldn't talk to me like that, but never followed through. It didn't occur to me to tell my parents, because in their eyes—in just about everyone's, certainly in his own eyes—he could do no wrong.*
>
> *When I turned 16, I became Glen's pet project. One day he offered me a ride home from a youth choir rehearsal. He drove me to a secluded area and made his intentions crystal clear. Every young girl longs to feel special, and he used that to his advantage, telling me how deeply he felt about me, showering me with gifts. The submission teaching was so entrenched in our church by that time that I really believed it was more spiritual to ask him for advice*

rather than my parents—with his knowledge of my deepest thoughts and struggles, he was able to skillfully manipulate me.

I was a naïve, weak-willed teenager whose desire to serve God got twisted into serving a God's man. If he wanted me, it must be right. Still, at first I asked him if what he was doing to me was "okay." He assured me it was, even quoted a few Scriptures. Satan, meanwhile, managed to warp the Word as I read it for myself—how about Hebrews 12:25…"See to it that you do not refuse him who speaks"…as a key verse for my growing deception?

Feelings of confusion must have been the Holy Spirit attempting to break through. Once Glen called and said he believed God was telling him to stop our relationship. When I hung up the phone I suddenly felt free—I hadn't even known I wasn't, you know? Five minutes later, he called back, said he knew he couldn't stay away. The bars clanged shut again.

When I dated a few guys my own age during this time, they seemed immature by comparison. Glen "protected" me from hurtful guys— if I were involved with him, they'd stay away. Then I met Joe, a new guy at church, and everything "clicked." Glen gave me some space (I realized by then that there were plenty of other members of the "harem") and eventually Joe and I got married.

Unfortunately, Glen got permission from Joe to visit me while Joe was at work, so Glen was soon back in the picture. My heart was being torn in two. I wanted to be a good wife, but I also wanted to be a good "sheep." People might think, "Why didn't you just tell him off or tell somebody?"—it makes me sick to think how deep into deception I was by then. I honestly didn't see a way out. One day I burst into tears when he approached me and he finally backed off. Emotionally, however, I felt no release, no freedom.

Finally Joe, bless his heart, had had enough "red flags" go up that he started asking questions. I told him the whole truth, hating the pain my words caused. As I poured out my heart, day after excruciating day, the scales fell off my eyes and I could finally see what sin had done to my life, my family, and to the Lord. My own sin, the parts of my relationship with Glen that were my responsibility, grieved God's heart but oh, the forgiveness he poured out, the unconditional acceptance. My love and appreciation for Joe deepened too, because of the compassionate way he responded.

The real turning point came when Joe and I confronted Glen and told him, in no uncertain terms, that his relationship with me was wrong, that it had never been right, and that he was never again to be alone with me. He was angry that I'd "confessed another person's sins." He even made it sound like I had pursued him! When he asked if we were leaving the church, Joe replied that church was about working things out, but we wish now that we had left, or at least told the elders what was going on. I'm pretty sure they already knew, but we should have followed through anyway. Convincing us he'd changed, Glen played the manipulation card one last time.

Things were settled as far as we were concerned, but there were others Glen was still involved with or who had never severed emotional ties from the past. When Glen died suddenly in a boating accident (soon after we'd talked to him) it was really difficult for them. Joe and I are so grateful that the Lord led us to speak up when we did.

13 Look at 2 Timothy 3:6-7. It isn't unusual for parents to lament the fact that their children are strong-willed. How does God use that trait as protection against danger?

_____

_____

_____

_____

_____

14 When Emily's parents eventually learned of her experience, they felt guilty. Joe asked her forgiveness as well—he ignored those "red flags" too long. As a 16-year-old, Emily was easy prey. But at 14, she had been cautious, righteously indignant at an inappropriate comment. What may have opened her up to deception two years later?

_____

_____

_____

_____

16 As a boy, Wayne sailed through catechism classes and confirmation, but the abuse occurred early enough that a real decision for Christ was, in his mind, out of the question. What would you say to him now, if you were a prison chaplain trying to win his heart for the Lord?

_____

_____

_____

_____

_____

17 The diocese slapped Father Bart's wrists numerous times before a costly lawsuit was filed and the reports were made public. When church government hides sin, what is communicated to the public? Should everyone who hid the abuse receive legal consequences as well? (Surely, there were already spiritual repercussions.)

_____

_____

_____

_____

18 Emily's unhealthy, submission-focused church provided an environment for Glen's particular area of weakness to thrive; other environments nurture other sins. Discuss enforced celibacy in the Catholic priesthood. What Scriptures support it? Which oppose it? Is it a viable excuse for sinful behavior?

_____

_____

_____

_____

_____

Happy endings are possible...

When Emily shares her testimony, occasionally someone expresses amazement that she's even a Christian, much less active in the church and happily married. "What Glen did was terrible—I don't excuse anything. Even though I wasn't totally innocent, he abused my trust and drew me into deception," she says. "But he had his own demons to battle. First and foremost—to the degree I understood what it meant—I wanted to serve God. God honored that, and protected me from things becoming even worse. Maybe it would be 'normal' to be very bitter—it's just God's grace and mercy that I'm not."

Father Bart was in many ways a caring and effective priest. Glen turned the hearts of many to the Lord. How could...and why *would*...God work through people who are simultaneously inflicting such suffering on others? When asked this question, a speaker nodded his head sadly. "I guess it's like this," he said. "God uses some of us *because* of our character, and some of us in *spite* of it."

Reflection & Encouragement

Statistically, an alarming number of young people are victims of sexual molestation and abuse each year; often a family member or close family friend perpetrates the abuse. The body of Christ is likened in the Bible to a family. We use terms like "brothers and sisters in the Lord." We're trained to honor leaders as spiritual fathers, to submit to their authority. But when they misrepresent God in order to use the weaknesses of others against them, and when the very ones God intended to help us find freedom to manipulate us until we are in bondage to *them*, the flock must take a stand.

The Joes in the church need to keep asking questions until they receive satisfactory answers. The Emilys need to speak up at the first hints of impropriety. Only then can the Waynes of the world...the hurting shells out there who equate God and the church and anything remotely related to Christianity with unspeakable shame...receive the healing and restoration they so desperately need.

There are *baaad* sheep, and *baaad* shepherds, but they need not have the power to turn us away from the Good Shepherd himself.

Closing Prayer

Father, our hearts break to think of the abuse taking place even now in your name or by those who call on your name. You grieve with us, for those sins nailed Jesus to the cross. Our sins did too—thank you for the forgiveness offered freely to everyone who believes and repents. Shine your light into our hearts and into our churches until every deed of darkness is exposed and banished in the name of Jesus. In his name we pray, Amen.

Week 7 Memory Verse

"Now the overseer must be above reproach...."

—*1 Timothy 3:2a*

Homework

❶ If you know someone who has been victimized, pray daily for him or her this week. Abuse *victims* struggle with issues such as guilt, doubt, anger, and bitterness—pray that with God's help, they are transformed into abuse *survivors*.

❷ Ask someone in church leadership about the current policies for avoiding and handling abuse.

❸ Take a look at one of the websites for "former Christians" and pray for those who post their stories. Each one represents personal pain.

❹ Breathe deeply and remind yourself that God is God. He has everything under control and is never surprised. He turns even the worst case scenarios into backdrops for his plans and purposes. Hallelujah!

❺ Do Week Eight to prepare for next week.

Forgiveness & reconciliation

"For if you forgive men when they sin against you, your heavenly Father will also forgive you. But if you do not forgive men their sins, your Father will not forgive your sins."
                                        —*Matthew 6:14-15*

Foreword to Week 8

One of the lessons the Lord has taught me in the six years following our youngest son's death is that once you've settled the issue of whether or not God exists, you're stuck. He is God; he can do whatever he wants, regardless of anyone's desires to the contrary.

If you consider yourself a Christian, you're stuck a second time—there is simply no way to avoid the responsibility we have to forgive those who hurt us...including fellow sheep.

A bumper sticker reads "Christians aren't perfect; they're just forgiven." The implication is that while Christians mess up like everyone else, unlike others, we have accepted the saving power of the shed blood of Jesus. This session will take it a step further. Our goal as Christians is to also be people who are forgiven *by one another...and who forgive one another.*

Remember Jesus' declaration that the world will only recognize our faith in him if we love each other? According to Drs. Dan Allender and Tremper Longman, "Love and forgiveness are equally bound together in all human relationships. I can't hope to ever love someone unless I am committed to forgive him. I can't hope to ever forgive him—that is, truly forgive him—unless I know the rich, incomprehensible joy of being forgiven."[14]

In Luke 7 we find the story of the sinful woman who anointed Jesus' feet with perfume, washing them with her tears, drying them with her long hair. When those watching rebuked Jesus for allowing her to touch him, he told them that her show of great love stemmed from a knowledge that her sins, yet many, had been forgiven.

When we agree with God that our own sins were (are) many, and that we are forgiven by the shed blood of the Lord Jesus Christ, we have an increased ability to love God, others, and ourselves. With the ability to love comes the ability to forgive.

If we choose to be followers of Christ, we must learn and practice the art of love and forgiveness, *especially* with fellow believers. If we refuse, we turn our back on the mercy we need from God and act in direct violation of his command. Yes, we've been let down by *baaad* sheep—but forgiveness is the key...the prerequisite...for getting past the hurts so that they no longer negatively affect us.

Opening Prayer

Gracious Father, we agree with your Word that we must love and forgive, but you know our frame, that we are but dust. The enemy has used those closest to us to hurt us deeply, knowing that forgiving them is the hardest thing you could ask. But you do ask. You command. Teach us to forgive. In Jesus' name we pray, Amen.

A working definition...

Doug Easterday travels throughout the world teaching at churches and missionary bases. Although many valid, even beautiful, definitions of forgiveness are offered on the shelves of Christian bookstores, his is particularly challenging to me:

> *Forgiveness is a decision I make to obey God and to walk as a lifestyle in a higher realm, no longer allowing other people's actions and attitudes to dictate my own but rather, releasing them to God while not requiring them to be accountable to me to "make it right." It involves a willingness to move in the opposite spirit from the one who hurt me, making sure that I am willing for God to use me as an unrestricted channel of his love for him or her.*

Forgiveness is a *decision* to obey God. It has much less to do with who has hurt us, how they hurt us, and why we don't want to forgive them, than it does with our personal level of commitment to Christ.

Forgiveness is a *choice* of lifestyle, an acknowledgement that forgiving someone is rarely done in one fell swoop, but lived out over a period of time as our heart softens, as the Lord reveals his plans and purposes, and as our spiritual maturity increases.

Forgiveness *releases us* from the power of those who hurt us. As long as we hold on to our precious personal pain, they're still in control. Simply seeing them makes our blood pressure rise. Having to speak to them brings a knot to our stomachs. Bitterness and unforgiveness can almost become a full-time job...the paycheck is dismal.

When we hold on to unforgiveness, embracing the hurt, it becomes a part of us. Eventually it transforms us into the likeness of the *baaad* sheep who let us down. Why would we willingly give them that power?

Forgiveness *releases those who have hurt us* so that the Holy Spirit can convict them of sin. When we don't demand repentance, change, or suffering as penalty for their offenses, God's power is released to work in their lives.

1   We usually think of intentional hurts when we think about the need to forgive. What about *unintentional* offenses? Discuss situations in which a person was completely unaware you were offended by something said or done. Was it easier or harder to forgive? Did you make the person aware of the offense?

_____

_____

_____

_____

_____

2   In many (if not most) conflicts, there is fault on all sides. Bill Gothard suggests listing the offenses of the person who hurt you, then listing your own.[15] For example, Jill deliberately misled Rachel (lying); Rachel told Melissa about the lie (gossip); Melissa "took up an offense" against Jill (unrighteous anger). Make lists for the three women, imagining what additional offenses might have

transpired. Then list situations where you have behaved similarly.

_____

_____

_____

_____

_____

You say poTAYto, I say poTAHto...

When Frank came in from the softball game to fetch chairs out of the school's cafeteria for the guest team, the principal stopped him. "They're trying to get things cleaned and set up now."

"But there's no place—"

"Leave the chairs, Mr. Morris." The lunch lady popped her head around the corner and quickly turned away.

Frank fumed as he made his way back to the game. He'd been looking out for the school's reputation, after all. And *Mr. Morris?* Since when were they not on a first-name basis?

After a restless sleep, Frank arrived at school early and stepped into the principal's office. "About yesterday—please forgive me," he said. "I thought I was doing the right thing, but I should've asked."

The principal nodded. "I shouldn't have spoken so sternly either. I appreciate you coming in to talk about it."

* * * * *

Kendra was puzzled. At choir practice Jimmi, a fellow tenor, had said something about another friend that Kendra knew to be false. Kendra felt so upset about the lie that she needed to leave practice early. As day followed miserable day, Kendra felt something should be done, but wasn't sure *what*.

Across town, Jimmi wasn't experiencing the "abundant life" either. She felt the distance with Kendra, but Kendra was the one who broke off the conversation, not her. Shouldn't she wait for Kendra to bring it up?

In Matthew 5:23-24, Jesus described an altar scene. While presenting a gift, you remember someone with something against you. According to Jesus, you should leave and be reconciled with that person before offering your gift to God.

In Matthew 18:15-17, he addressed a second situation: If another believer sins against *you*; you should go and talk to him. If reconciliation is possible, great; if not, return with witnesses. If that doesn't work, go to the church. Somehow we have gotten away from the idea that the church was intended to help us on a daily basis, to help us resolve problems with one another, but Jesus gave us the model.

Who should make the first move in a conflict? *You.* Either Frank or the principal, either Kendra or Jimmi, could biblically seek out the other. It's a matter of who is more in tune to the urging of the Holy Spirit, who is more sensitive to the harm caused, or maybe even whose spouse offers reminders that things need to get straightened out.

3 Conflict is sometimes a matter of perception—a deep hurt may have been caused unknowingly. Without bringing it to the hurtful person's attention, can there ever be a resolution? God's Word talks much about praying for those who hurt you (Matthew 5:44, Romans 12:14) and overlooking offenses as much as possible (Proverbs 12:16; 17:9; 19:11). How do these verses apply?

_____

_____

_____

_____

_____

4 At the same time, taking responsibility for one's own actions in the matter shows humility and may diffuse anger. Frank felt his actions were justified, but apologized anyway. What would you have done? Discuss Romans 12:18. Could either man have used this as motive for action?

_____

_____

_____

_____

_____

5 Frank was embarrassed that another staff member heard the principal reprimand him. How might things have escalated had Frank discussed it with her?

_____

_____

_____

_____

_____

6 Kendra recognizes that Jimmi said something about someone else that was false (i.e., "bearing false witness"). How should Kendra respond to Jimmi about the matter?

_____

_____

_____

_____

_____

7 If Jimmi isn't sure that what she spoke was truth, what should be her response?

_____

_____

_____

_____

_____

8 What other verses would encourage her to seek Kendra's forgiveness?

_____

_____

_____

_____

9   If Jimmi is more troubled by the distance than Kendra, what should be Jimmi's response? (See Matthew 5:23-24.)

_____

_____

_____

_____

_____

Who are you to tell me...

Gina wasn't part of the church class studying a particular book, but when she became aware that its entire premise was fraudulent, she discussed it with the minister.

The next Sunday Bernie, the study group's leader, charged at her while she was still in the parking lot, his face red with anger. "How dare you talk down my class!" As he continued to rant, it seemed to Gina that he was angrier because a *woman* had questioned his materials than anything else.

Gina prayed…and cried…and prayed some more. Reading the Psalms brought tremendous comfort. She remembered hearing of personal trials in Bernie's life that probably added fuel to the fire. Instead of responding with anger or self-pity, she began interceding for him regularly.

Months later, she and Bernie happened to walk down a church hallway together. "I've forgiven you, you know," she said softly.

"For what?" Bernie replied gruffly. "*I'm* the one who should be doing the forgiving around here."

"Well," Gina stared up at him, "there's no time like the present!"

10 Gina trusted the minister to work out the materials question with the group leader, and trusted the Lord to deal with Bernie's heart. Should she have gone to Bernie initially? Why or why not?

_____

_____

_____

11 Confrontation isn't Gina's strong suit, but with one sentence, Bernie's arrogance and anger was forced into the spotlight. What were his choices at that moment?

_____

_____

_____

_____

_____

"Sorry" doesn't cut it...

Forgiveness is neither wishy-washy nor magical. Some thirty years ago, at a skating rink with my future husband, I mentioned that another fellow had made an offensive remark. David took the young man aside and demanded an apology. When he complied, I said airily, "Oh that's okay."

But it *wasn't*. He had been out of line; my feel-good response offered absolutely no motivation to change his future behavior. Saying he was sorry simply revealed a desire to avoid David's left hook, not genuine repentance.

* * * * *

Luann was recovering from the shock of moving with two toddlers when her husband's business transferred him to Alaska, requiring yet another move. "Winter arrived in September, snow by October. By mid-December the sun rises around 11 A.M. and sets by 1!" Separated from friends and family, they looked for a church home to fill in some of the gaps.

Soon she and her husband found not only a congregation with which to worship but another couple there from their home state with whom they forged a close relationship. Unbeknownst to Luann, the other wife had been the special friend of Nora, "the most controlling woman on the planet." Luann was designated Public Enemy #1—*very* public.

"Nora was very active, headed committees, led Bible studies, you name it. She had to be the center of attention, forever running the show. Everywhere I went she was there, cold as the weather. During one ladies' meeting, she brought up the problem of cliques, practically pointing her finger at me—we'd just started going there! She was so hateful I ran out in tears. Later I learned that when I left, Nora rolled her eyes and made some comment about what a 'crier' I was."

Perhaps the Holy Spirit convicted Nora as she continued to lead the meeting; perhaps someone took her aside and talked to her. Whatever the motivating factor, Nora approached Luann, confessing she was jealous of the easy way Luann had made friends. Comparing herself and her marriage to Luann, she'd come up short and gotten angry. "Can you ever forgive me?"

In their book *Bold Love*, Drs. Allender and Longman say that "biblical forgiveness is never unconditional and one-sided. It is not letting others go off scot-free…(enabling them) to do harm again without any consequence. Instead, (it) is an invitation to reconciliation, not the blind, cheap granting of it."[16]

Luann learned more during her first Alaskan winter than just an appreciation of sunshine. "Christians come from all different walks of life, at different levels of spiritual maturity. As a leader, it took humility for Nora to reveal her weakness—God showed me my own faults and gave me an ability to pray for her that I wouldn't have thought possible."

Have you ever noticed that when Satan condemns, he speaks in general terms, making true repentance impossible? How do you repent for being a bad person, a terrible friend, an ineffective mother, an awful example of a Christian? When the Holy Spirit *convicts*, on the other hand, he is painfully specific: You shouldn't have taken that. That was an unloving thing to say. You must be more consistent with your discipline. You need to ask your brother to forgive you.

When Nora compared herself with Luann, Satan whispered lies into her ear: You'll never be that happy. You'll never have another friend like the one she stole. When she submitted to the Lord, however, conviction cut to the chase—jealousy and anger.

12 Can someone be forgiven without repentance? Look at Jeremiah 15:19, Luke 13:3, Acts 2:38.

Refer again to Doug Easterday's description of forgiveness:

Forgiveness is a decision I make to obey God and to walk as a lifestyle in a higher realm, no longer allowing other people's actions and attitudes to dictate my own but rather, releasing them to God while not requiring them to be accountable to me to "make it right." It involves a willingness to move in the opposite spirit from the one who hurt me, making sure that I am willing for God to use me as an unrestricted channel of his love for him or her.

13 Can or should we choose to forgive despite the other person's attitude of repentance? (See also Mark 11:25, Matthew 18:21-22.)

14 "I'm sorry" is an inadequate request for forgiveness. Discuss other examples of inadequate and adequate requests for forgiveness such as "If I hurt you...."

15 Read Matthew 7:3-5 and discuss how Jesus used relative size in the illustration. Hold a quarter up to your eye—it is "big" enough to cover the face of the person across the table. Viewed by that person, however, its size is insignificant. How does this principle apply to forgiveness and offenses?

_____

_____

_____

_____

_____

What it's not...

If you cut off my hand, God can give me the grace to forgive you...but I'm still missing a hand. There are *always* consequences for misbehavior. An apology—even a sincere apology born of righteous repentance—doesn't necessarily mean that consequences will not be experienced.

Forgiveness also doesn't mean that an offense will be forgotten, or that the offender will be trusted as in the past. The daughter of a sexual predator may (with divine grace) forgive her father, but she would be wise to press charges and ask to be placed in another relative's care. People who have lied, gossiped, or stolen shouldn't expect their victims to develop short-term memory loss! In the previous section, Luann didn't become Nora's new best friend and ride off with her into the sunset—the Lord simply enabled them to relate in a godly manner. That was enough.

Nor is forgiveness a one-time act. Emily, whose story we read in the last session, was at a small group meeting years after Pastor Glen died. Singing with her eyes closed, she suddenly heard his voice joining the others. "A wave of what can only be described as pure hatred went through me," she said. "I thought I'd forgiven him completely, but apparently there was still work to be done."

As with any task requiring work, forgiveness is a process. When I referred (in the second session) to a notorious gossip as "Satan," I showed that the process in me is still incomplete! The woman's actions and attitudes (at least at that moment) still controlled mine. There has been *progress* to the *process*, but I haven't completely "arrived."

16 Think of a time your feelings were hurt as a child. Does the memory of the incident still cause pain, or has increased understanding of the event coupled with the passage of time enabled you to view it differently?

_____

_____

_____

_____

_____

17 Disappointment has to do with expectations. Read Proverbs 11:23 (the Hebrew for "hope" can also be translated "expectation"). Is God ever disappointed? If we give up our right to expectations, would this decrease the number of times we must forgive?

_____

_____

_____

_____

_____

Privacy policies...

In the midst of Janie and her husband's marital struggles, she was asked to step down from the worship team so she'd have more time at home. "This is my oasis—I *need* this," Janie cried. "Will you at least explain things to the team?" The worship leader declined, and months later, apologized privately for his error in judgment, inviting Janie back...right after the other keyboard player broke her wrist.

* * * * *

Newt stood before the congregation and confessed to being an adulterer. The sin had occurred years before, in another place, but he "just needed to get it off my chest." His wife sat in the front row, head bowed as he shared.

* * * * *

"I've been so resentful of you," Judy tearfully told Monica. "You're everything I'd like to be. Will you forgive me?" Monica was dumbfounded. All this time, she had regarded Judy as a close friend.

When the government passed the HIPAA law to protect medical information, every health provider and pharmacy had to go with the flow, spending an inordinate amount of time and money implementing new "privacy rules." God's ways are far more logical: if a sin is against God, one should ask his forgiveness. If the sin is against another person, *that* person should be asked. Only if the sin was public, must confession be public as well.

18 Janie's worship leader held her up for possible misunderstanding, even slander, by other team members, who might wrongly assume she was being penalized for some indiscretion. How might he have communicated his decisions to the team, in Janie's presence, in order to build unity and compassion?

_____

_____

_____

_____

_____

19 Newt's wife was hurt by his public confession. Even though she had remained faithful, she felt that his infidelity reflected badly on her too. Because she was involved, should Newt have obtained her consent? Would the need to share openly be different if it were a recent offense? If Newt was in leadership?

_____

_____

_____

_____

_____

20 Judy had successfully kept her resentment to herself, but she was convicted of her sin. What damage did revealing this to Monica do?

_____

_____

_____

_____

_____

The reward of forgiveness...

If repentance is the work one does to receive forgiveness, reconciliation is the reward. Complete reconciliation isn't always the result, as we'll see in the next session, but when it is, it's a truly glorious "God thing."

Evie slammed down the phone without letting her Christian friend and co-worker Charlotte finish. She just couldn't listen anymore—the words were so hurtful, the criticism of her performance on the job so groundless, Evie was certain the damage to their relationship was irreparable.

"Charlotte's birthday was coming up and she had an extra-special weekend planned—we'd prayed and talked about it for weeks. Suddenly I was out of the loop," said Evie. "When she came up to me at work, I turned my back on her. I wouldn't speak to her, wouldn't return phone messages."

A few days later while on her way home from work, Evie felt compelled—"That's the only word for it; I *had* to call"—to call Charlotte on her cell phone. "'It's over,' I told her. 'Not our friendship, the conflict! The Lord showed me I had to lay it aside completely, like it had never happened. In myself, I never could have done it, but the Holy Spirit just washed the bitterness away. It was nothing short of miraculous, in my book.'"

* * * * *

John left his wife and children for the weekend to pray about leaving them for good. Another woman had entered his life, one that better complemented his interests and talents. In her he had finally discovered the helpmate God intended every man to have. For decades, he had waited for his wife to willingly fit into her role—hadn't he waited long enough?

He'd forgiven his wife for hurting him so many times in the past; he trusted her walk with the Lord and figured that eventually, she'd forgive him for this. As for the kids—better a happy father some of the time than a miserable one all of the time, right?

As he reflected on the Lord's direction, it suddenly hit him who he was, and who his wife was. "God called us to be one.

Mr. and Mrs. John Barker. He never called us to be anything *else*." The next day he returned home and gathered everyone for a family meeting. With tears in his eyes, he said simply, "I'm staying." Of all the things to be worked out and worked through, they needn't fear he would leave. Ever.

21 Charlotte may have planned to apologize, but Evie "beat her to it" by asking forgiveness for her response. Read Romans 12:9-21. One translation reads "Outdo one another in showing love." Discuss the ways Evie obeyed these verses.

_____

_____

_____

_____

_____

22 John's family, while rejoicing at his decision, took a "wait and see" attitude until he proved (through his lifestyle and choices) that his renewed commitment was real. Discuss some of the things you would be looking for in the same situation.

_____

_____

_____

_____

_____

Reflection & Encouragement

It bears repeating: if we're Christians, we're stuck; albeit stuck for our good. Jesus is Lord. We've been bought with a price and are no longer ruler of the roost. The one who IS in charge has made it clear...painfully so...that we are called both to love one another and to forgive.

We don't have to like the ways in which *baaad* sheep let us down. We don't even have to like *them*. But when fellow believers hurt us (and they will, if they haven't already) we are commanded to take specific steps to make things right.

The Hebrew *shalom* is translated "peace," but its full meaning is much richer. It says, in effect, that there is nothing between us. There are no shadows in our relationship behind which negativity can hide. May the day come when we are able to look into the eyes of each brother and sister who has hurt us and say sincerely, "*Shalom.*"

Closing Prayer

Loving Father, thank you for reconciling us to yourself through the shed blood of Jesus Christ. And thank you for giving us the ability, through that same blood, to be reconciled with our brothers and sisters. Teach us to forgive, because it is your command. Teach us to forgive, so that we may be forgiven. Teach us to forgive, so that those who have hurt us don't continue to control us. Teach us to forgive, so that we may learn to love. In Jesus' name, Amen.

Week 8 Memory Verse

"For if you forgive men when they sin against you, your heavenly Father will also forgive you. But if you do not forgive men their sins, your Father will not forgive your sins."

—Matthew 6:14-15

Homework

❶ Oh, you can just guess what's coming, can't you? Make a list of people you need to forgive, and a second list of people who may need to forgive you. You know what to do!

_____

_____

_____

_____

_____

❷ Do Week Nine to prepare for next week.

What to do when Week 8 crashes & burns

"If [your brother] refuses to listen even to the church, treat him as you would a pagan or a tax collector."

—Matthew 18:17

Foreword to Week 9

Mysteries may abound in the Bible, but God's take on forgiveness isn't one of them. If another believer sins, he laid out certain steps for us to initiate in the whole forgiveness/restoration/reconciliation package. And if we're aware that we have offended someone *else*, Jesus said to go make it right. He never specified whether or not the offense was justifiable; he didn't include subsets or special clauses for offenses that are premeditated, in poor taste or hilarious in nature. If you see sin, do this. If you're the offender, do that. All quite simple, right?

But we're dealing with people, remember. What is simple on paper is not necessarily *easy* to walk out. The issue of forgiveness is paramount to our relationship with God—if we don't forgive, he won't either—but it is also a process, hence the need to adopt a *lifestyle* of forgiveness.

Most of the time, if we're honest with each other, we would rather chew on things than deal with them. Our goats eat a little, then sit down and let their stomachs work on the grass awhile until their systems can handle the nutrients more efficiently. We like to ruminate over offenses the same way—relive what was done *just one more time* before addressing the matter of obedience to Jesus' directions.

Yet…when we finally take that deep breath and dial the phone number of the person we've hurt…or go to meet with the *baaad* sheep who hurt us by sinning against us…we're setting ourselves up for being let down *big* time if we assume that now the sun is going to come out and birds will sing. When you do everything "by the book" (*the* Book) only to crash and burn, what are your options *then*?

Opening Prayer

Abba Father, there are times we want to crawl up in your lap and sob until we use up all our tears. So much of the time we have to deal with our own wrongdoing—that's hard enough! But when we obey you and still "inherit the wind" of fury from brothers and sisters, it's almost more than we can bear. Teach us what our responses should be. Help us to say, "Father, forgive them even though it seems they know exactly what they're doing." In Jesus' name we ask, Amen.

If you'd just...

Sondra lay very still on the couch, listening carefully to the Bible study held in her home despite intense suffering. Her husband wanted her to stay in bed—doctors felt the end was near—but she was stubborn. "I want to hear. It's a distraction from the pain."

As the group dismissed to fellowship around the snack table, a woman came and sat down, taking Sondra gently by the hand. "My heart grieves that Satan is winning this battle!"

Sondra's heart sank, looking for someone nearby to rescue her from what she sensed was coming. As the other woman's voice affected an instructional tone, Sondra closed her eyes and began praying silently. There was a faith conference coming up...one of the speakers had a special gift...she would be glad to take her...by his stripes we ARE healed...never give up....

* * * * *

Franklin set down the phone. Another friend from church had called to "encourage" him to contend the divorce. The guys at work seemed to understand his situation better than his Christian brothers! Millie had made his life miserable for years, refused counseling, openly despised him. He had to answer for his own faults, sure, but Millie had abandoned the family on her own accord.

Maybe with some distance, the Lord could work in her heart. In the meantime, Franklin mused, it would be so refreshing to get a call or e-mail saying, "I'm praying for you, buddy. Just wanted you to know we love you."

1   Sometimes what we consider to be the "sin" of a brother or sister is simply that of following another path than we would take ourselves. How do we differentiate between the pride of *not understanding** and the humility of restoring another to fellowship with the Lord?   (*How many times, when discussing another's decision, do we preface it with "I just don't understand how he could…"? What we're really saying is that the person is wrong and our stance is correct…pride.*)

_____

_____

_____

_____

_____

2   Sondra's "friend" was offended by her sickness, Franklin's "brothers" by his broken marriage. Look at Philippians 2:20. How do Christians promote their own interests of health, stability, financial security, etc. by imposing personal standards on others?

_____

_____

_____

_____

3   A child may be told to "mind your own business", but the Bible implies that at least in some situations, we are to be our "brother's keeper." Look at Romans 14:15; 2 Corinthians 2:5-11; Hebrews 3:12-13. Does that necessarily mean we are to always "set them straight"? What, actually, does it mean?

_____

_____

_____

_____

The Ambush...

Mitch was in a quandary. A small group of church members had invaded his personal life and taken a course of action so beyond his comprehension, so outside the realm of anything he knew how to deal with spiritually, that forgiveness was like "trying to pick up a slip of paper in a gale. I would reach for it, barely touch it, only to have a new gust blow it down the sidewalk again," he said.

Attempts to deal with the matter "just between me and God" were not successful. He knew unforgiveness wasn't a viable option, but his daily mantra of "Father, forgive them for they know not what they do" wasn't cutting it. In desperation, Mitch requested a meeting. "We were 'family,' after all. When they understood the result of their behavior, I figured they'd apologize, relationships would be restored, and we'd all grow through the experience. Talk about *naïve!*"

After complicated explanations and excuses were offered, the conflict seemed to be getting ironed out. Assumptions had been made based on faulty logic and an unhealthy dose of trying to "fix" things. While it was sadly obvious to Mitch that his feelings had been overlooked in favor of the feelings of others, at least everything was on the table.

"If we'd said our good-byes at that point, things might not've deteriorated," Mitch remembered. The group was well aware that Mitch was still reeling from a recent tragedy—"I just presented too easy a target to ignore. They seized the opportunity to tell me everything that was wrong with me," he shuddered, the memory stirring him again, years after the fact. "Apparently, there was quite a lot."

In all fairness, Mitch understands now that raw emotions rendered him "hypersensitive," but the realization that people he trusted...people he thought loved him...would not only *ignore* his pain but also add to it "filled me with such anguish I couldn't talk—I could hardly breathe. My family still refers to that day as The Ambush."

4 Mitch prayed about creative ways to deal with his emotions following The Ambush. "Laughter has medicinal value," he said, "so I've got a collection of favorite funny movies to turn to." Scientific studies would agree, as would King Solomon. Read Proverbs 17:22. Discuss instances where comedy has helped combat drama in your life.

_____

_____

_____

_____

_____

5 How might Mitch "flesh out" Hebrews 12:14-15?

_____

_____

_____

_____

_____

6 Other approaches Mitch tried in the area of "anger man-agement" included anonymous gifts for his Ambushers, vigorous exercise, even yoga. Discuss the merits of each.

_____

_____

_____

_____

_____

Ambush, revisited...

Following an "ambush" of my own, a woman who had said some very hurtful things to me sought me out in my backyard a few weeks later to make peace—true *shalom* peace, nothing between. Still disagreeing with a decision I'd made, she had reached the conclusion that our relationship was more important to her than being "right."

No divine wind swept through the yard to right all wrongs just because she sought reconciliation, but it was a start. It takes time to rebuild relationships—perhaps it will take the rest of our combined lifetimes—but the first stones were laid that afternoon.

When one of Mitch's accusers moved to another state, he half-expected a letter or phone call. "The guy prays—I'm sure of it," Mitch said. "In all this time, why hasn't the Holy Spirit reminded him that he offended me?"

And the others who verbally attacked him...have they never "offered a gift" at the altar only to hear the Lord clear his throat and say, "Oh and by the way—remember the day you verbally beat up that wonderful son of mine?" That's the way Mitch imagined it, at any rate!

Maybe God *has* spoken, many times. Ultimately, *baaad* sheep answer to no one but him. Our responsibility, on the other hand, is two-fold: forgive and love.

7 Jesus said we are to forgive a brother multiple times in a single day for the same offense. We sometimes get bent out of shape over a *single* offense in an entire *lifetime*! Read the account again (Matthew 18:21-35). How has the Lord shown mercy to us? Can we pay back what we owe?

_____

_____

_____

_____

8 Jesus said that after we try (and fail) to reconcile with an offending brother privately (regarding sin), we should take one or two witnesses along and try again. If he still fails to listen, we should announce the offense to the church. If he still won't listen after dealing with the matter *this* drastically, we are to "treat him as you would a pagan or a tax collector" (Matthew 18:17). What does that mean? How did Jesus treat pagans and tax collectors? In your experience, do offenders/offendees usually follow Jesus' guidelines for conflict resolution?

_____

_____

_____

9   Referring again to Matthew 18:21-35. What should be your response, in your own life, to another believer who sins against you? Is forgiving contingent upon the offending brother's repentance? If you can think of any examples, please share them with the group.

_____

_____

_____

_____

_____

The goal is coal...

Mia couldn't get past the negative thoughts and feelings she was having for Renee, a younger woman at church. There was nothing to talk about with Renee, since there had been no actual offense. In fact, Renee had been nothing but kind to her, yet Mia was increasingly aware of deep resentment toward her.

Remembering something her grandmother had taught her as a child, she decided to shower Renee with anonymous acts of love and generosity. You can guess what happened, can't you? Oblivious, Renee delightedly received unsigned notes of encouragement and flowers delivered to her home. And by leading Mia to go through the *motions* of a loving attitude, God was able to breathe a loving attitude into her heart.

10   Paul quoted Proverbs 25:21-22 in the letter to the Romans. Read his words in context (Romans 12:9-21). Scholars are divided as to the actual meaning of the phrase "heap burning coals on his head"—while it sounds like a punishment (and burning coals were used as such, apparently), it may also refer to the sharing of "fire" from one's home to help a beggar start his own. Discuss the interpretations and how they might apply to the idea of responding to *baaad* sheep with kindness.

_____

_____

_____

_____

_____

Know when to hold, know when to fold...

Despite the fact that he managed to accumulate a thousand wives, King Solomon is often regarded as the wisest man in history. His timeless words in Ecclesiastes 3:1-8 (no pun intended) have much to tell us as we encounter *baaad* sheep in the church:

> *"There is a time for everything, and a season for every activity under heaven...a time to plant and a time to uproot...a time to tear down and a time to build...a time to embrace and a time to refrain, a time to search and a time to give up...a time to be silent and a time to speak...."*

If an offense only scratches the surface, forgiveness and love are no great challenges. Other times, the hurts reach to the marrow. Jesus gave definite directions for the road to reconciliation, but as we saw, even those do not always have the desired effect. (Or haven't yet. There's no fat lady involved, but "it ain't over" till it's over.)

There may come a time to uproot, to leave, to separate from a source of contention in order to give ourselves time to heal...a time to—in a sense—"give up"...give up the notion that people have to like us or treat us the way we want to be treated, give up the hope that offenders will repent on our time schedule, give up an environment that constantly reminds us of pain.

11 When the reason for leaving a church is a resolve that certain *baaad* attitudes and actions are longer going to be tolerated, do you think members should be given the opportunity to announce their reasons for leaving a congregation?

_____

_____

_____

_____

12 Division, as we saw in Session Three, can be a positive thing. Look at 2 Thessalonians 3:14-15. Discuss what the relationship would look like.

_____

_____

_____

_____

A lesson from Luke...

Cool Hand Luke, that is. Despite its age, one of the lines from this film has consistently appeared on "favorites" lists. When Luke escapes from prison and is surrounded by authorities, the warden deadpans, "What we have here is a failure to communicate."

That's often the problem of the church in a nutshell.

Near neighbors Maggie and Laura became best friends. Maggie professed a belief in God; Laura hoped their friendship would draw her closer to the Lord. "I was selfish," Laura admits, "fearful I'd offend her. I shared my struggles with her, so who was I to question *her* choices?"

Laura said nothing when Maggie publicly criticized her family or got drunk. She also didn't mention the sexual advances made by Maggie's husband Tony—advances she did not immediately refuse. "Not to excuse anything, but my husband was a workaholic—I just wanted to feel wanted and loved. That's all he wanted too, really." Fortunately, they decided to end any semblance of romance before things got out of control. *Un*fortunately, the decision came just as Maggie learned of the relationship.

Still bitter about an affair years before (also with one of her friends), Maggie refused to sit down with Laura and talk things out. Laura recalled, "It hurts to know that I hurt *her* and all I can do is pray, and stay out of her way. She thinks I betrayed her with her husband, but the real betrayal was being a coward. If I had really loved her with *Christ's* love, I would've confronted her a long time ago about her destructive behavior. Maybe she would have rejected me *then*, but it would have prevented me from making such a mess of things."

13 Laura's "failure to communicate" godliness to her friend led to being cut off from *all* communication. Re-read Matthew 5:27-30. How could Jesus' words serve as *encouragement* to Laura today, who has no contact with Maggie or her husband, no mutual friends…she even moved out of the neighborhood.

_____

_____

_____

_____

_____

14 Read Luke 12:47-48 and discuss its relation to Laura, who openly professed Jesus, and Maggie, an admitted backslider. Laura believes she is most responsible for what went wrong—do you agree? Why or why not?

_____

_____

_____

_____

_____

15 2 Corinthians 6:14 is often used in discussions about marriage. Read the verse in context. How might this apply to Laura's situation? Look at 1 Corinthians 15:33 and Psalm 1:1 and discuss reasons we should pursue or avoid particular relationships.

_____

_____

_____

_____

_____

Reflection & Encouragement

Abuse victims are encouraged to delay confrontation with their abusers until they can come from a position of strength. When *baaad* sheep hurt us, we would do well to heed the same advice, building up our spiritual strength in prayer and meditating on the Word of God. We should also pray about the timing of our conversations and whether or not we need to take someone along as a witness. Although we can be hopeful, expecting *baaad* sheep to respond in a godly way, or expecting them to give accurate accounts of our meeting later, would be unwise.

When we are the offenders, prayerful preparation is even more important. Acknowledging that we were wrong without offering excuses, attempting to place blame elsewhere, or reaching for justification is contrary to human nature. We need to be clothed with the divine nature, to "put on love" (Colossians 3:12-14), before we venture forth.

And whether we are, in this particular instance, the *baaad* sheep or the victim of *baaad* sheep, remember that even if we say the right words, do the right things, hold our mouth the right way (sometimes successful reconciliation seems to hang on such trivialities) the results may still be...at least today...less than satisfactory.

Most of the time when conflicts occur, problems continue because Christians do not follow through on Jesus' steps. If we have done all we know to do in order to be reconciled...all we're capable of doing at the time...and that shalom peace remains elusive, we must turn it over to God and trust him with the results. He may lead you to discontinue activities that would put you in near proximity to the others involved. Don't think of it as giving in to failure, but as removing the potential for further pain.

What then? 'Consider (Jesus) who endured such opposition from sinful men, so that you will not grow weary and lose heart' (Hebrews 12:3).

And again, 'A man reaps what he sows. The one who sows to please his sinful nature, from that nature will reap destruction; the one who sows to please the Spirit, from the Spirit will reap eternal life. Let us not become weary in doing good, for at the proper time we will reap a harvest if we do not give up. Therefore, as we have opportunity, let us do good to all people, especially to those who belong to the family of believers' (Galatians 6:7a-10).

Closing Prayer

Awesome God, we can be so stubborn that it amazes us when we actually obey your Word...and we expect to get good results when we do! When we don't, we get discouraged. Help us to see things (and people) from your perspective, trusting that you know the end from the beginning and that in your good time, you will make all things right and new. Give us the grace and patience to respond to disappointing results in a godly way. In Jesus' name we ask these things, Amen.

Week 9 Memory Verse

"...if [your brother] refuses to listen even to the church, treat him as you would a pagan or a tax collector."

—*Matthew 18:17*

Homework

❶ If you have not already taken steps to make restitution or to attempt reconciliation with the people you listed in last session's homework, pray for guidance and wisdom in following through.

❷ Send an anonymous card or gift to someone who hurt you in the past.

❸ Write a prayer list of people who have hurt or been hurt, using names from personal experiences as well as those shared in the group and from this workbook. (God knows their real names, even if you don't.) Ask the Lord to continue to work in each heart.

_____

_____

_____

_____

❹ Do Week Ten to prepare for next week.

Taking a backward step of faith

"Let us consider how we may spur one another on toward love and good deeds. Let us not give up meeting together,...but let us encourage one another—and all the more as you see the Day approaching."

—Hebrews 10:24-25

Foreword to Week 10

There are *baaad* sheep all around us, Christians who let us down in ways both big and small. If we sincerely desire to follow Christ, however, our response must be forged out of love with the end-result of forgiveness. There are times when an appropriate response includes confrontation, even laying relationships aside. But "giving up" a friendship, group, or church doesn't mean giving up on God...or his other children.

The church at large is not really an *organization*, although many believers treat it as such. If we can just implement this particular program, if that group will just act in a more Christ-like manner. The goal of an organization, once up and running, is *maintenance*. Therefore, performance becomes Job One.

The church, however, is likened to a body. It is, in a very real way, an *organism*, living, breathing, all members (theoretically, at least) functioning as a unit. The goal is *ministry*. Because we also have a "very real" enemy who tries to thwart that ministry, we experience roadblocks to ministry at every turn.

People struggle with fear, pride, tradition, ideas regarding social status and denominational concerns, gender bias, biblical ignorance, cultural differences, narrow-mindedness, conflicting career choices...all of these can keep us from ministering within the church and beyond. What we have focused on in this study is the way the hurts of those around us and our subsequent unforgiveness also keep us from doing God's will—from being the effective ministers he created us to be.

My hope and prayer for this study is that even those who have been hurt the most deeply by Christians will retain…or *regain*…the desire to pursue Christ in the fellowship of other believers. That doesn't mean sitting, Sunday after Sunday, beside the person who spread lies about you all over town, singing choruses through clenched teeth and inviting a stroke as your blood pressure skyrockets.

It *does* mean seeking the Lord for the ability to forgive that person. Until you take that step of obedience, you actually allow him or her to control your life Remember, forgiveness does not excuse a person's offense against you, but it does remove the negative effect he or she (or the offense, or any combination thereof) continues to exercise over you.

Opening Prayer

Abba Father, we need the fellowship of other Christians—your Word says we do. The hurts of believers have sometimes caused us to withdraw, either emotionally or physically. Draw us back. Give us a hunger for one another, a hunger for the unity that Jesus prayed we would achieve through the Spirit. In his name we pray, Amen.

Exit, stage left...

Our last major exit from a congregation left the family in a state of limbo. We tried various flavors of churches around the area—although each warranted tics in the "good things about them" column, none felt like *home*.

A couple of small, intimate fellowships just starting out were so small they felt almost claustrophobic—was there really a need for yet another church of only a handful of members? Perhaps…but we weren't at a place where *growing* a church was our priority—we were hurting. We needed a strong, spiritual-meat-providing congregation that would give us time to heal while aiding the process with acceptance and love.

The happy-happy-friendly church was large enough to have the programs we'd need for the grandkids that lived with us, but when the worship leader chastised all in her range of sight who weren't smiling and clapping, our still-grieving hearts sank. Was there no room for people who were filled, through no fault of their own, with sorrow and suffering? Did God want us to just suck it up and grin in order to fit into someone's mold of effective Christianity? We thought not.

A long-time friend pastored a long-established denominational church doing a grand job of keeping up with his new ideas. Our love for him and his family could...if we let it...outweigh the things that weren't right up our alley...but then we were led to move out of state, before those relationships had a chance to gel.

When you get right down to it, how *could* a church fill our need? "Home" was a church we helped start, a place where we'd invested time and tears to see the Lord fulfill his purposes. The fact that it became a place of deep hurt precipitated our departure, but didn't erase the shared history.

We seemed destined for perennial visitor-ship, never moving beyond the superficiality for which many Christians settle as a normal church experience but which couldn't possibly provide the depth of commitment and fellowship God intends. Finally—about the time I decided I was willing to go *anywhere* as long as biblical truth was offered—the Lord answered our prayers through a wonderful congregation in our new state.

A new home. New job. New roles. New church.

Is it perfect? Well, did you hear the story about not looking for a perfect church, because once you become a member, it *isn't* any more? Our present church is no exception—*baaad* sheep may lurk in the shadows of smiles there too. In time, one or more of them may even let me down. And because I know how truly ugly I can behave when I'm operating in the flesh, I know that—given time—I will hurt others and be a *baaad* sheep myself.

The risk of being hurt, even deeply, still exists. I would be *safer* if I avoided the church setting altogether. But I wouldn't be happier. And I certainly wouldn't be more *obedient*.

1 Discuss moves you have made from one church to another, even one class to another. What prompted the moves? Were the results 100% positive, 100% negative, a mix?

2 Sometimes change is imposed on us. A new teacher leads, a new pastor arrives. What are some ways these changes can be made more easily?

3 As a grieving family, our expectations for comfort (that dirty word again!) may have worked against us, at least in measure, in finding a congregation that "fit." What other expectations could prevent visitors from feeling at home?

Trust those people?

Aaron had the pastor and congregation convinced he was a model husband; his wife Heather felt there was no one in whom she could confide. He verbally abused her, was unfaithful, lied constantly—in time, his true colors would no doubt be unmasked in the church setting, but Heather felt she was running *out* of time. She had a child to consider; the last time Aaron had thrown a fit, he'd put a gun to her head in front of the boy. "It hurt that everyone took Aaron's side and kept telling me to 'just submit.' I was the one who brought him to church in the first place! He's such a manipulator, he had them all snowed. When I finally left him, I had to leave the church too. I didn't trust them to care for *me*."

It took awhile, but Heather finally found a church that would love her and her son *in spite of…*all the things that had brought them to that place.

* * * * *

Mallory had been through two messy divorces and was struggling to make ends meet for her children and herself. They lived in a small town where everyone knew everyone else's business (and talked about it), but she craved the stability and support of a church.

"I thought it would be nice to attend with my mother, even though the worship was dead as a doornail. When I walked into Sunday School, one of the regulars took one look and said, 'What are *you* doing here?'" Mallory had no idea what prompted the comment, but she felt so unwelcome, she never went back.

In time, Mallory found a congregation that would welcome her unconditionally…the way the Lord welcomes her.

4 Both Heather and Mallory were experiencing a period of weakness due to their circumstances. *Ideally*, what should the response of believers have been to them?

_____

_____

_____

_____

5 Read James 1:27. How does the verse apply to Heather and Mallory's situations? Discuss other people you know who could be categorized as "orphans and widows." Are their churches exhibiting "pure and faultless" religion?

_____

_____

_____

_____

6 Both women eventually found churches that nurtured their walks with God. "Found" implies action on their part—searching, seeking, wanting. Discuss what might have happened had they decided "church" just wasn't worth the trouble.

_____

_____

_____

_____

_____

7 During conflict, adrenaline shoots through our bodies with the "fight or flight" reflex. It's normal, from a natural standpoint, to respond to hurt by either hurting back or escaping. Read Romans 8:1-17 and discuss the *spiritual* standpoint.

_____

_____

_____

_____

_____

Complaints Department now open...

Sometimes what prompts us to consider pulling up stakes and heading elsewhere isn't anything as defined as the rudeness Mallory encountered. Sometimes we fall into the trap of making assumptions or taking up offenses toward others.

Millicent's husband wasn't paid to direct the choir, but that didn't affect his dedication. Eager to serve the church with her talents as well, Millicent filled in for the secretary one summer. One day as she typed some letters, another church member came in to talk with the pastor.

"They were in the room next to me and didn't shut the door. There was no way to avoid hearing. The whole appointment centered on criticism of the music program in general, and my husband, in particular! I mean, he had every right to vent to the pastor, but I was *right there*. It made me wonder if maybe it wasn't intentional."

Millicent wasn't sure what to do—leave for lunch? That would require notifying the pastor. Close the door? Confront them? For 45 minutes, the tirade continued, after which the man left without speaking to Millicent. The pastor never mentioned the conversation.

"Then it became all about what to do with the information—tell my husband? Talk to the pastor?" Satan began planting suspicions. Surely the man knew who she was. It had been planned for her to hear, so she'd repeat the conversation to her husband. The pastor had probably invited the man to come when Millicent would be there because *he* was dissatisfied with the music program. Maybe they were right. Maybe her husband was doing a bad job. They should just leave.

Millicent wasn't the one to decide, of course; her husband, the spiritual leader of the home, would have to make that choice. She spoke to him, and was surprised by his response: "That guy complains about *everything*! Don't worry about it."

8   Millicent suffered in silence, caught off guard by what she considered a blatant disregard for her feelings—by both the man berating her husband's volunteer efforts and by the pastor. Discuss optional responses.

_____

_____

_____

_____

9   Millicent's husband laughed when she shared with him that night: "That guy complains about *everything*! Don't worry about it." Look at Proverbs 11:9. How does being aware of another's area of weakness help keep offenses in perspective?

_____

_____

_____

_____

10 Relationships must be nurtured in order to reach "safe" levels. What does Millicent's response tell you about her level of relationship with the pastor? The church member?

_____

_____

_____

_____

_____

Don't make me look bad...

Curt excitedly accepted a position with a major Christian recording studio, viewing it as more ministry than job. "I was especially looking forward to meeting the 'big dogs,' the tour headliners who impact the whole world."

What Curt soon discovered, to his chagrin, was that *baaad* sheep aren't confined to pews and pulpits—they stand on platforms as well, performing for thousands, signing autographs, and appearing on television. "Most of the artists I meet are just what their music leads you to expect—men and women of God whose *walk* matches their *talk*. Some of them, though...."

Curt felt let down, personally offended by the behavior of people with whom he'd never even spoken. "I considered quitting and going to a secular company. It took me a while to realize that the message can be valid even if the messenger is flawed—and my job is to get the message out. Working here has taught me a lot about the importance of character, but also about trusting God to work through anyone."

Curt was tempted to leave a Christian business, rather than a church, because he was let down by the *baaad* sheep he encountered there. "When I started out, I coveted the positive influence they could shine on me. Since reality hit, I can only pray that God will use me to influence *them*."

* * * * *

Carol had lunch from time to time with a group from work. When a church group she also knew began lunching near "their" booth once a week, her co-workers were quick to complain: The "good Christians" rudely left the tables together for the waitress to take care of. The tips were pathetic.

They were picky about their orders. That's why you won't find *me* in church. Yada, yada, yada.

Carol said nothing. The next time she saw the church group, however, she slid into the chair next to one of them. "Would you do me a favor?" she whispered.

"Sure," he said, perhaps thinking she wanted to share a prayer request.

"This is the only opportunity you'll get to witness to some of these people, and they're watching you like hawks. When you leave, would you mind putting the tables back? And leave a big tip for the waitress? She works really hard—I'd really appreciate it."

Soon, Carol noticed a decline in criticism. Carol praises God—"All it took was a little reminder that their behavior could turn people off to so much more than their little group."

11 Curt was offended that representatives of the Christian elite (in his mind) didn't hold up under close examination, but he also didn't want to "judge." Look at Jesus' detailed warnings concerning the teachers of the law and Pharisees (Matthew 23). Sometimes we treat the *recognition of sin* as a sin. What Scriptures support our ability, even our responsibility, to recognize and address sin around us?

_____

_____

_____

_____

12 Public awareness of a celebrity's faults can reflect badly on anyone associated with the celebrity. How did loyalty to Curt's company, love for his job, and even pride come into play?

_____

_____

_____

_____

13 Carol felt a connection both to the Christian group and to the co-workers who were offended by their behavior. Contrast Matthew 5:9 with Luke 12:51. In dealing with spiritual conflict, how do we decide which actions are appropriate for which situations?

14 Some of Carol's friends pointed to the rudeness of Christians as the reason they didn't go to church. What excuses have you heard from others? Do they stand up under scrutiny?

15 Do things like the group's rudeness serve to distract nominal believers or non-believers from the real issues of salvation?

Great expectations...

Following our son's burial service, we went to our church for a covered dish luncheon they had thoughtfully provided. I don't care where you go or how many *baaad* sheep there may be out there, there will also be a dedicated army of women with the gift of hospitality and organization, beloved Marthas ready to put on a spread with little or no notice.

One lady took me aside. "I've been here preparing, so I wasn't at the funeral," she said tenderly. "I just want you to know that I will be there for you from now on." We hugged, wiped our tears, went on to speak to others.

Six years later, she has yet to make so much as a single phone call. This was no spiritual slouch, either! A ministry leader, popular, esteemed by all...how could she let me down like that?

At the five-year mark, we were in the process of settling into a new home in a new state. Anniversaries bring an increase of emotion, and as I remembered the woman's earnest commitment afresh, I wrote her a letter...which I never sent, not after my husband read it.

"In all this time," he asked, "how many times have you called *her* and asked for help?" His question, by the way, was met with a combination of murmuring and looks that could kill. But he was right (he usually is, darn it).

I had *expected* the woman to reach out to me with comfort and assistance. She had—if we give her the benefit of a doubt—expected me to reach out to her when I had a need. Had I done that, I'm sure she would have indeed "been there." Is she a *baaad* sheep? I don't know. But I was let down by one of those "failure to communicate" mishaps that abound.

16 Re-read Proverbs 11:23. *People* let us down when *our own expectations* let us down. What steps can we take to eliminate expectations from our thinking?

_____

_____

_____

_____

_____

17 Paul's beautiful description of *agape* (selfless and godly) love implies the expectation of another's best: "[Love] always protects, always trusts, always hopes, always perseveres" (1 Corinthians 13:7). What verses might temper an unreasonable (and therefore *let-down*able) attitude?

_____

_____

_____

_____

_____

18 We expect, at times, more from others than we would want them to expect from us. Has someone ever put you on a pedestal? What was his or her response when you fell off? (Assuming you have, by now.)

_____

_____

_____

_____

_____

Shaping up...

Someone came up with an acronym for service in the church which handily fits our focus: SHAPE, standing for S(piritual gifts), H(eart or passion), A(bilities), P(ersonality), and E(xperience). God has created each of us uniquely, composites of all those ingredients which can, if channeled properly, lead us into the ministry of his choosing.

Where do the hurts of *baaad* sheep fit? E- experience. Even the hurts we have known in the past can "shape" our future ministry. Someone who has been devastated by nasty gossip, for example, will be more tuned in to the possibility of his or her words causing damage and may be more apt to choose a ministry such as counseling, where trust is of vital importance.

Emily's molestation by her pastor could easily have soured her on Christianity, on church, on God. "I keep coming back to the fact that we're all sinners, saved by grace," she said.

"The fact that Glen had a problem with lust didn't exclude the fact that he was an anointed teacher."

It surprises us to realize that Glen motivated Emily, and many others, to press harder into God, to pursue a closer relationship with the Lord, even while he struggled with his own sins and shortcomings. But time and time again, throughout history, God has used fallen humans to achieve greatness.

From Adam and Eve, to Noah and his drunkenness, to Abraham and his desire to make God's will happen, to David and his lust for Bathsheba, to Solomon and his alliances with foreign women, to Esther and Jonah and their initial fears, to Peter and his betrayal, to Paul and his misdirected enthusiasm, to men and women ever since who have struggled with their own flesh while being used of God to affect their world...God's purposes and plans *will* be accomplished despite those who hurt others.

We have the opportunity to let those experiences in which we have been let down lead us into areas of ministry to help *others* who have been let down. Do we want to be a *part* of what he's doing, letting him use those hurts to help heal...or will we let the sins and weaknesses and foolishness of others *prevent* us from joining in the heavenly dance he has choreographed from the beginning of time?

19 There are many examples in the Bible of people who hurt others and yet were still loved by God and used by God in mighty ways. Why do we expect the humans we encounter on a day-to-day, or Sunday-to-Sunday, basis to be perfect?

_____ _____

_____

_____

_____

_____

20 A friend of mine, fairly high up the food chain in the military, says his commander gets frustrated with him because he loves conflict. Where others try to avoid it at all costs, my friend sees conflict as an *opportunity* to work with God in a situation and in the hearts of those involved. How would adopting this attitude help us deal with *baaad* sheep, and possibly transform a church (or any group, actually)?

_____

_____

_____

_____

_____

21 Look at 1 Corinthians 12, especially verses 4-5 and 27-31. As a Christian, this means you! Have you found your ministry (or ministries)? Now look at the very last part of the very last verse... "And now I will show you the most excellent way." What is it?

_____

_____

_____

_____

_____

22 A novelty T-shirt reads "Plays well with others." Think of similar slogans that would be helpful in recognizing the weaknesses in fellow believers so that we could more easily avoid hurt: "Easily Offended", "Caution—Wears Emotions on Sleeve", "Habitual Gossip", etc.

_____

_____

_____

_____

_____

23 Now think of some slogans that we could wear to display a redemptive pursuit to the above slogans: "Somewhat Forgiving", "Mostly Self-Controlled", "Patient—If Only Mildly Provoked", etc.

_____

_____

_____

_____

_____

Reflection & Encouragement

I hope someone came up with "Loves one another" in that last exercise. Even if it's wishful thinking, even if that hasn't been our experience 100% of the time with *baaad* sheep associated with church, we need to keep going back to Jesus' command. It is *that* simple and quiet command we are to obey, not the loud emotional responses to the very real hurts we experience that clamber for attention.

We're a motley crew, we followers of Christ. Thrust together on Sunday mornings, and maybe other times during the week, each of us is a combination of heredity, environment, hurts, struggles, triumphs, hopes, dreams, spiritual maturity, ideas, intelligence, hormones, sins, and moods. When you think about it, it's amazing we're not *all baaad* sheep more often, letting one another down left and right.

This realization certainly provides insight into the urgency of Jesus' words. For the crowning glory of his message to his disciples, he commands exactly what is the most difficult—to love. He *knows* we won't succeed at love, even within church walls, without supernatural assistance—he has no expectations, remember? He knows the end from the beginning and is therefore never disappointed. But he orchestrates the songs of our lives so that we come to the end of ourselves…and turn to him. When we do, he *is* always there for us.

The hurts we have suffered by the words and deeds of *baaad* sheep are part of our training as overcomers. Until we respond to hurts *according to God's word*, they will continue, because God loves us too much to leave us as he finds us. Even when we learn a lesson, hurts will still be our lot in life because we are imperfect people in an imperfect world. That doesn't excuse *baaad*ness—it simply acknowledges that it exists.

By identifying the *baaad* sheep around us, learning to bear with or avoid their behavior, and forgiving their offenses, we are no longer controlled by them. We are free to "press on" as Paul wrote:

"Not that I have already obtained all this [surpassing greatness and righteousness in Christ], or have already been made perfect, but I press on to take hold of that for which Christ Jesus took hold of me...I do not consider myself yet to have taken hold of it. But one thing I do: Forgetting what is behind and straining toward what is ahead, I press on toward the goal to win the prize for which God has called me heavenward in Christ Jesus. All of us who are mature should take such a view of things. And if on some point you think differently, that too God will make clear to you. Only let us live up to what we have already attained" (Philippians 3:12-16).

Amen.

God is God and we are not. For reasons we don't always understand, he wants us to fellowship with other believers. He calls us to corporate worship. He says that in the midst of "two or three" (Matthew 18:20), he is there...and he's also with two or three hundred.

We need the insights others can give us. Their support can sustain us in times of trouble. If anyone reading this has been so hurt that he or she has given up on church altogether...if you've been so hurt that you can't believe another Christian actually cares...let me just say that as a representative of the body of Christ—poor representative though I may be—I'm sorry you have been hurt. I ask your forgiveness. But please...come back. Take a step back to the "first love" you once found within a church's walls and among its people.

Don't give up on all of us because you've run into a few *baaad* sheep.

The rest of us need you.

Closing Prayer

Father, teach us by your Holy Spirit to love and forgive. Teach us to bring our hurts to you and lay them at your feet. Teach us to see one another through your eyes. Teach us to recognize and hate sin while retaining the ability to love the sinner. Draw us closer to you and as each draws closer to you, we will be drawn closer to one another. Lead us into all truth, and lead us to the people who will best further your plans and purposes for us. In Jesus' name we pray, Amen.

Week 10 Memory Verse

"Let us consider how we may spur one another on toward love and good deeds. Let us not give up meeting to-

gether…but let us encourage one another—and all the more as
you see the Day approaching."

—Hebrews 10:24-25

Homework

❶ If you have stopped attending church, a particular
Sunday School class, singing in the choir, etc. because of
unresolved hurts, address them now. What is God trying
to teach you in the situation? Where does he want to lead
you?

_____

_____

_____

_____

_____

❷ If you know someone who has stopped going to church,
pray about ways to reach out to him or her and then follow through. It is easy for people to fall through the
cracks—don't let their departure be due to your lack of
caring.

❸ Share your own baaad sheep stories…and how the Lord
helped you show love and forgiveness. E-mail
EllenOfGillette1@aol.com or write to me c/o CarePoint
Ministries, Inc., P.O. Box 870490, Stone Mountain, GA
30087.

"Better is the end of a thing than the beginning."

—Ecclesiastes 7:8a, KJV

End Notes

[1] Pat Zukeran. "Abusive Churches". (Additional information from: Ronald Enroth, *Churches That Abuse* [Grand Rapids, Mich.: Zondervan, 1992]):1993. http://www.leaderu.com/orgs/probe/docs/abuse-ch.html

[2] Karen (Leininger) King. "Healed of Church Abuse", *Communion with God Ministries*: March 12, 2002. http://www.cwgministries.org/Healed-of-Church-Abuse.htm

[3] M. Scott Peck, M.D. *People of the Lie—The Hope for Healing Human Evil* (New York: Simon and Schuster, 1983), 10.

[4] Elizabeth George. *A Woman's High Calling* (Eugene, Oregon: Harvest House, 2001), 41.

[5] Dr. Henry Cloud and Dr. John Townsend. *Safe People* (Grand Rapids, Michigan: Zondervan, 1995), 59.

[6] George. *Op. Cit., Growth and Study Guide*, 30.

[7] Gorton Carruth and Eugene Ehrlich. *The Harper Book of American Quotations* (New York: Harper & Row, 1988), 100.

[8] *Ibid.* Quoted from Elbert Hubbard's *The Roycroft Dictionary and Book of Epigrams* (1923), 100.

[9] Carmen Renee Berry. *When Helping You is Hurting Me* (New York: Harper Paperbacks, 1988).

[10] Bill Cassada. "God of the Heart...Church of the Mind: Part 4 (Shepherds or Shepherding)", © 2005 The Lion's Heart Ministries, Inc. http://www.thelionsheart.org/article_Godoftheheart_Part4.html.

[11] "Controlling Personalities in the Church: The Warning Signs" http://www.wittenberggate.net/.

[12] Oswald Chambers. *My Utmost for His Highest* (Grand Rapids, Michigan: Discover House Publishers, 1963), February 7 selection. See also http://www.myutmost.org/index.html.

[13] Dr. Henry Cloud and Dr. John Townsend. *Op. Cit.*, 197.

[14] Dr. Dan B. Allender and Dr. Tremper Longman III. *Bold Love* (Colorado Springs, Colorado: NavPress, 1992), 42.

[15] Bill Gothard, *Institute in Basic Youth Conflicts — Research in Principles of Life* (1979).

[16] Allender. *Op.Cit.,* 162.

Printed in the United States
213201BV00002B/3/P